BEST
EDITORIAL
CARTOONS
OF THE YEAR

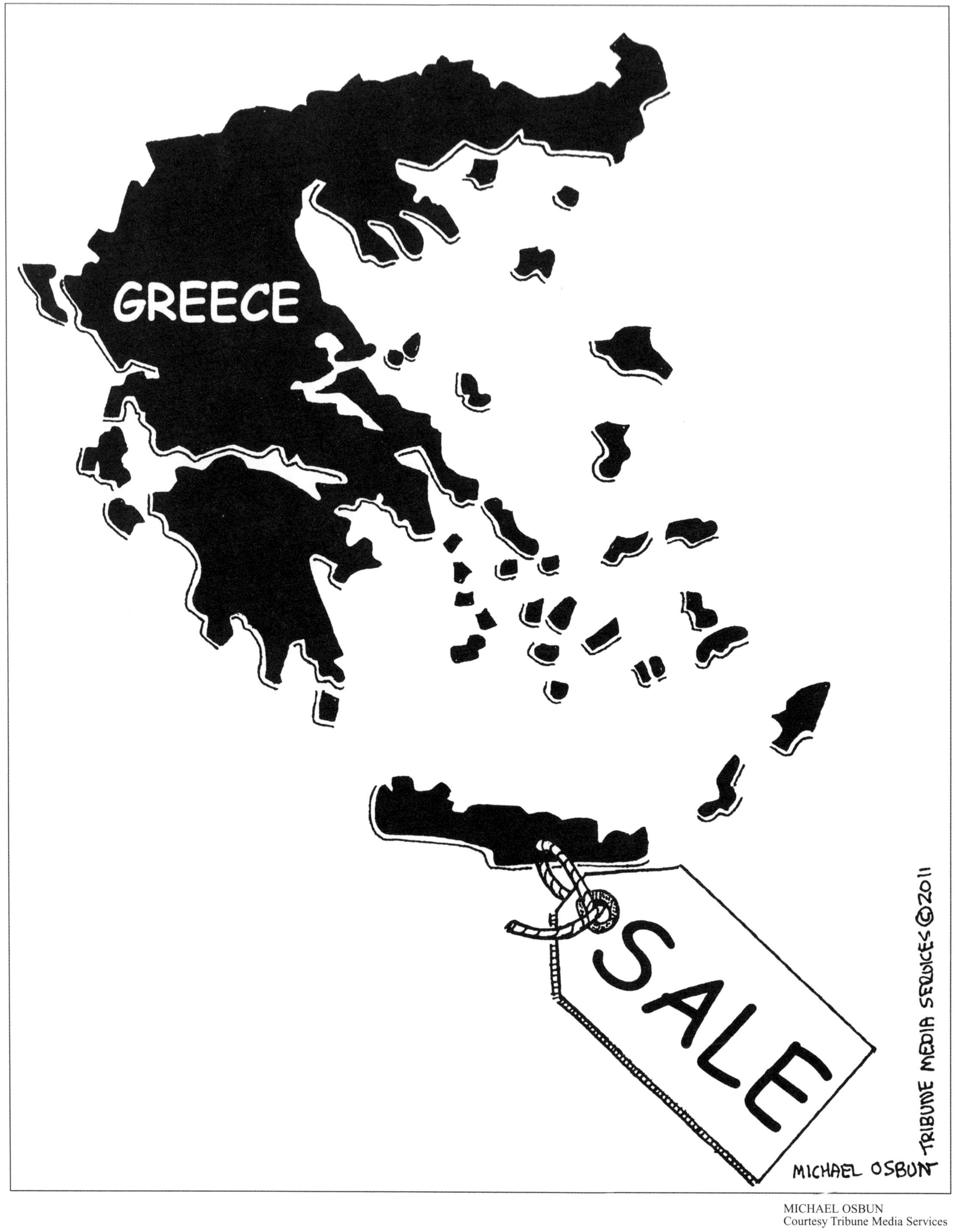
GREECE
SALE
TRIBUNE MEDIA SERVICES ©2011
MICHAEL OSBUN

MICHAEL OSBUN
Courtesy Tribune Media Services

BEST EDITORIAL CARTOONS OF THE YEAR

2012 EDITION

Edited by
CHARLES BROOKS

PELICAN PUBLISHING COMPANY
Gretna 2012

Library of Congress Serial Catalog Data

Best Editorial Cartoons, 1972-
Gretna [La.] Pelican Pub. Co.
v. 40 cm annual—
"A pictorial history of the year."

United States—Politics and Government—
1969—Caricatures and Cartoons—Periodicals.
E839.5.B45 320.9'7309240207 73-643645
ISSN 0091-2220   MARC-S

Printed in the United States of America
Published by Pelican Publishing Company, Inc.
1000 Burmaster Street, Gretna, Louisiana 70053

Contents

Charles G. Brooks, Sr.
1920–2011

For 40 years, in 40 volumes, Charles Brooks compiled and edited the annual you hold in your hands. On September 29, 2011, as this 2012 edition of *Best Editorial Cartoons of the Year* was in the final stages of preparation, he passed away.

He was our colleague, our friend, and a tireless advocate of the cartooning art. A past president of the Association of American Editorial Cartoonists, he was an award-winner in his own right. He was the proud recipient of thirteen Freedom Foundation awards, a national

A typical Brooks cartoon, celebrating the greatness of the United States of America.

Veterans of Foreign Wars award, two Vigilant Patriot awards, and the National Sigma Delta Chi Award for editorial cartooning presented by the Society of Professional Journalists.

Throughout his career he emphasized the positive about his United States of America. To him, the United States was, and remains, a bastion of freedom, a shining light of leadership for the rest of the world. He championed individual rights, personal liberty, and one's responsibility to his fellow man. His cartoons regularly reflected those principles.

Chuck was born with a love for drawing. While other youngsters dreamed of being cowboys, or baseball players, or firemen, Chuck wanted to be a cartoonist—specifically, an editorial cartoonist for his home-state Alabama newspaper the *Birmingham News*.

After service in World War II (which included a D-Day landing on Utah Beach in Normandy), he achieved that dream, and for 38 years his work graced the pages of the Birmingham newspaper.

He knew what he believed, and believed in, but he was also tolerant of dissenting views, a quality often in short supply in contemporary society.

Thus ends a remarkable career—38 years of practicing his art and 40 years as an editor and chronicler of the best works his fellow cartoonists. That combination of achievements as artist and editor is not likely to be surpassed.

Award-Winning Cartoons

2011 PULITZER PRIZE

GRIDLOCK

MIKE KEEFE

Editorial Cartoonist
The Denver Post

Born in Santa Rosa, California; grew up in St. Louis, Missouri; graduate in mathematics from the University of Missouri at Kansas City; cartoonist for the *The Denver Post,* 1975-present; named John S. Knight Fellow at Stanford University; past president of the Association of American Editorial Cartoonists; three-time winner of the John Fischetti Competition, including the 2011 honor; previous winner of the National Headliner Award, the Sigma Delta Chi Award, and the Berryman Award; author of three books.

2011 JOHN FISCHETTI COMPETITION

MIKE KEEFE

Editorial Cartoonist
The Denver Post

2010 SIGMA DELTA CHI AWARD
(Awarded in 2011)

STEPHANIE MCMILLAN

Editorial Cartoonist
Code Green

A political cartoonist since 1992; self-syndicates *Code Green,* a weekly editorial cartoon focusing on the environmental emergency; draws the comic strip "Minimum Security" for Universal Uclick; author or co-author of three books; work has appeared in various textbooks and anthologies and in several volumes of the Opposing Viewpoints series; founding member of Cartoonists with Attitude, 2006.

MIKE PETERS

Editorial Cartoonist
Dayton Daily News

Born in St. Louis, Missouri; received Bachelor of Fine Arts degree from Washington University, 1965; joined art staff of *Chicago Daily News,* 1965; served in the U.S. Army, 1966-67; editorial cartoonist for the *Dayton Daily News,* 1969-present; cartoons syndicated nationally since 1972; his award-winning "Mother Goose & Grimm" comic strip, created in 1984, is syndicated in more than 500 newspapers throughout the world; has 28 titles of the Mother Goose & Grimm series in print; winner of the Sigma Delta Chi Award, 1975, and the Pulitzer Prize for editorial cartooning, 1981; previous winner of the National Headliner Award, 1983, 1988, and 1993; awarded Doctor of Humane Letters by the University of Dayton, 1998; cartoons syndicated by King Features Syndicate.

2011 THOMAS NAST AWARD

MIKE PETERS

Editorial Cartoonist
Dayton Daily News

2011 HERBLOCK AWARD

TOM TOLES

Editorial Cartoonist
The Washington Post

Graduate of State University of New York at Buffalo; started career as cartoonist for the *Buffalo Courier-Express,* later working for the *Buffalo News,* the *New York Daily News, New Republic* magazine, and *U.S. News and World Report;* editorial cartoonist for the *Washington Post,* 2002-present; winner of the Pulitzer Prize for Editorial Cartooning, 1990; among other honors, he has been the recipient of the National Headliner Award, the John Fischetti Competition, the H.L. Mencken Award, and the Thomas Nast Award; author of a book for children, *My School Is Worse Than Yours.*

BEST
EDITORIAL
CARTOONS
OF THE YEAR

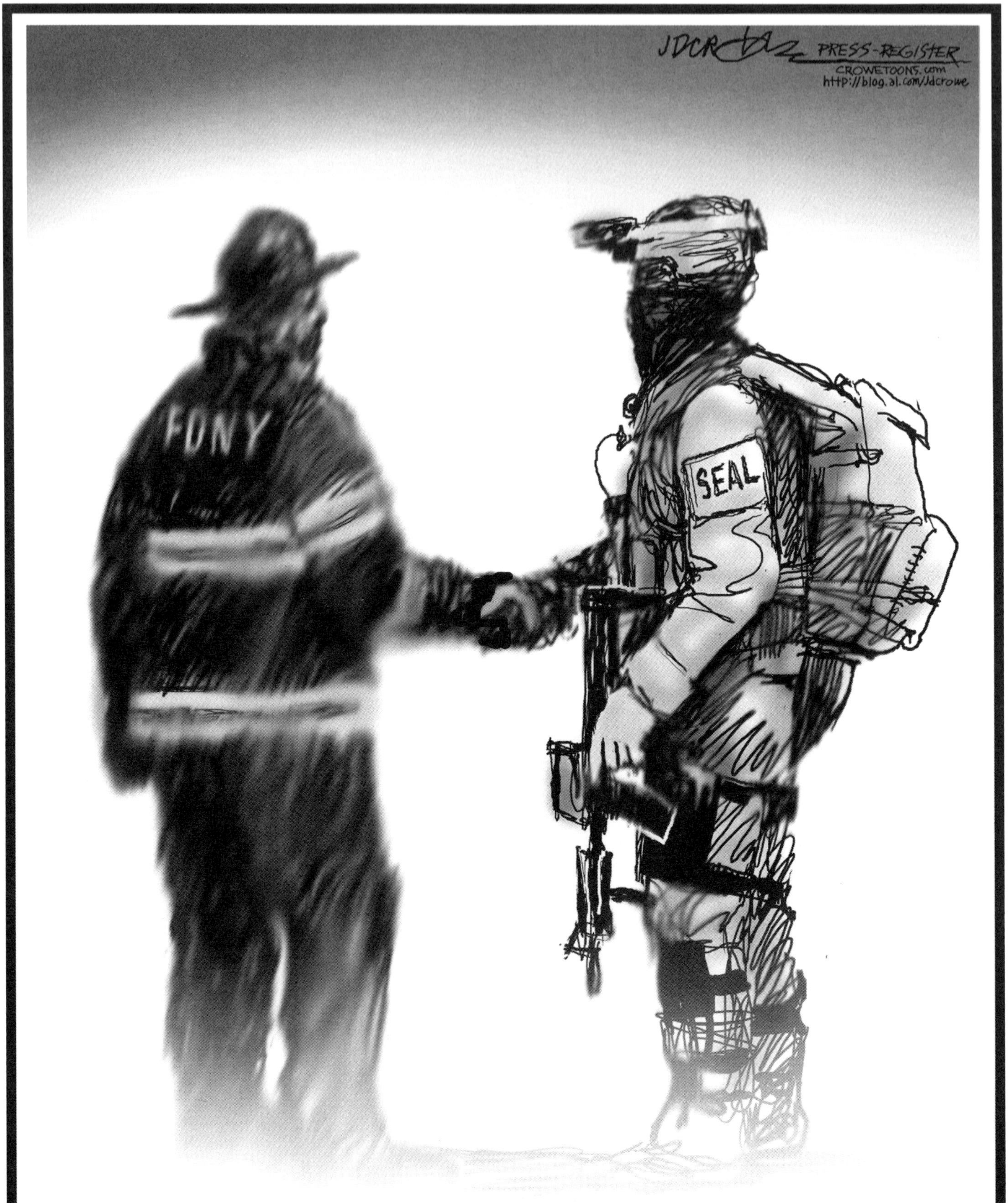
JDCROWE PRESS-REGISTER
CROWETOONS.com
http://blog.al.com/Jdcrowe
FDNY
SEAL
GROUND HERO

J.D. CROWE
Courtesy Mobile Press-Register

Getting bin Laden

Members of Navy Seal Team 6 raided Osama bin Laden's compound in Pakistan and killed the world's most wanted terrorist. The speedy, precision attack was a testament to the efficiency of the Seals. Bin Laden's body was buried at sea to avoid having a shrine for al Qaida sympathizers to rally around.

Bin Laden, the leader of al Qaida, had planned the attacks on 9/11 and was the subject of a manhunt by U.S. forces for 10 years. Bin Laden's compound in Pakistan stood right under the noses of the Pakistani military. The incident made lawmakers wonder just how faithful an ally Pakistan was in the war on terror and whether Pakistan should continue to receive billions in U.S. aid.

The incident was seen as a coup for President Obama, earning him praise from all points of the political spectrum and a temporary bump in public approval.

JEFF DARCY
Courtesy The Plain Dealer (Oh.)

CHARLIE DANIEL
Courtesy Knoxville News-Sentinel

BARRY HUNAU
Courtesy Jerusalem Post

NEIL GRAHAME
Courtesy Spencer Newspapers

STEVE MCBRIDE
Courtesy The Reporter

DAVID DONAR
Courtesy donarfilms

19

TIM DOLIGHAN
Courtesy Dolighan Cartoons

RUSSELL HODIN
Courtesy HODIN INK

CHUCK LEGGE
Courtesy Artizans.com

20

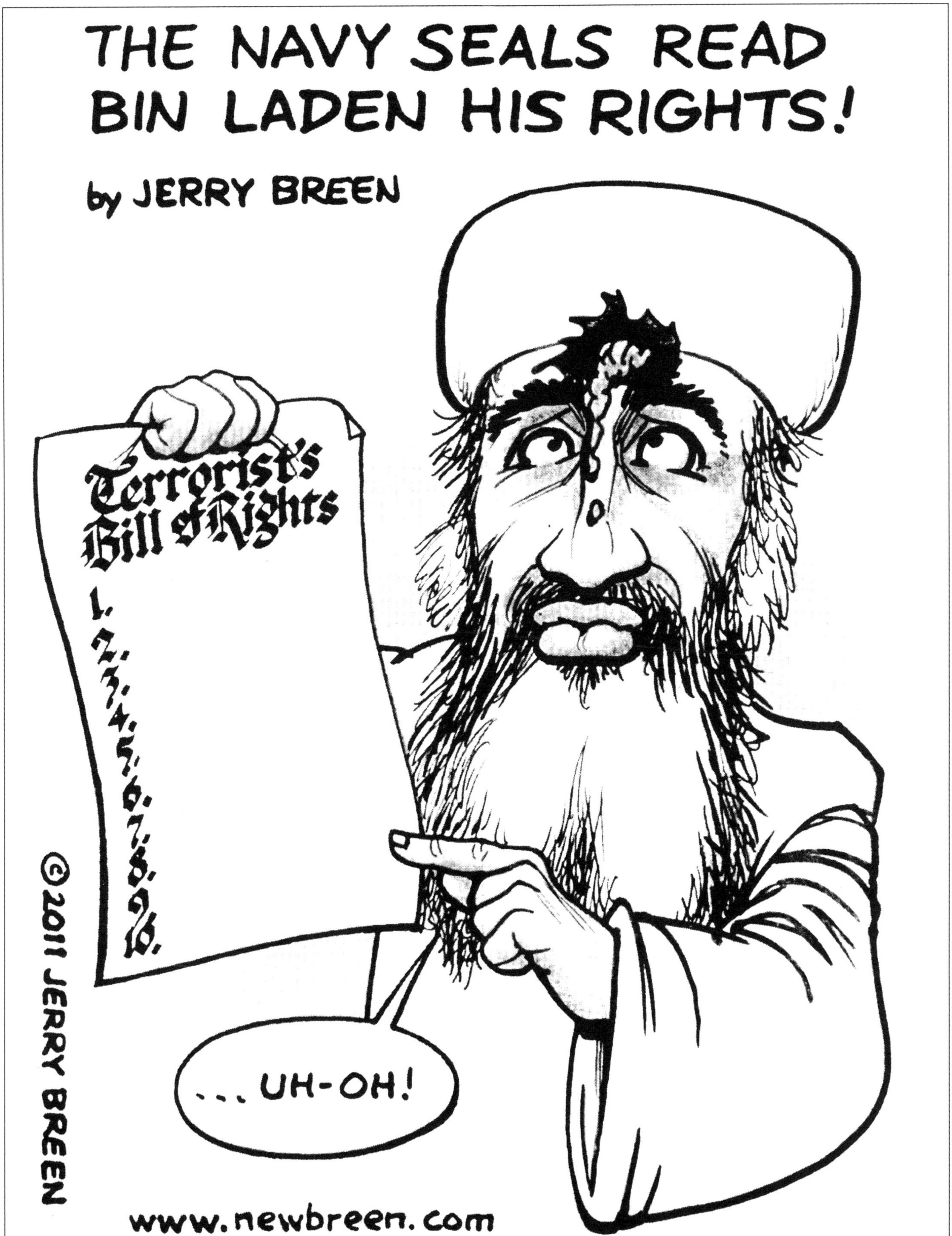
THE NAVY SEALS READ BIN LADEN HIS RIGHTS!
by JERRY BREEN
Terrorist's Bill of Rights
1.
2.
3.
4.
5.
6.
7.
8.
9.
10.
...UH-OH!
© 2011 JERRY BREEN
www.newbreen.com

JERRY BREEN
Courtesy newbreen.com

DAN ROSANDICH
Courtesy danscartoons.com

ED HALL
Courtesy Baker County Press (Fla.)

MARK STREETER
Courtesy Savannah Morning News

JIM MCCLOSKEY
Courtesy The News-Leader (Va.)

DAVID HORSEY
Courtesy Hearst Newspapers

23

TOM STIGLICH
Courtesy Northeast Times (Pa.)

CHRIS BRITT
Courtesy State Journal-Register (Ill.)

DONALD E. LANDGREN JR.
Copyright Worcester Telegram & Gazette Corp.
Reprinted with permission.

JOSEPH O'MAHONEY
Courtesy The Patriot Ledger

PAUL FELL
Courtesy Artizans Syndicate

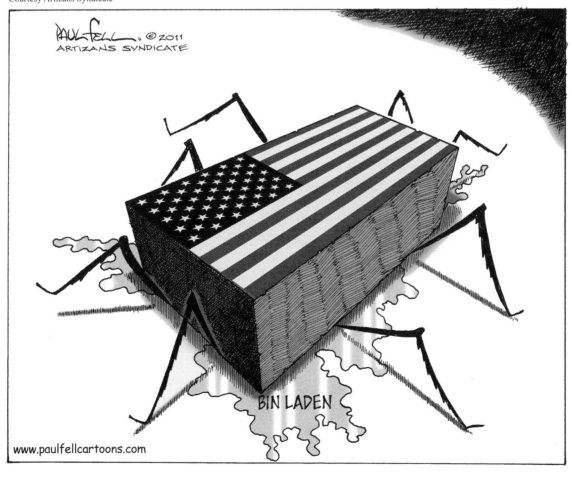

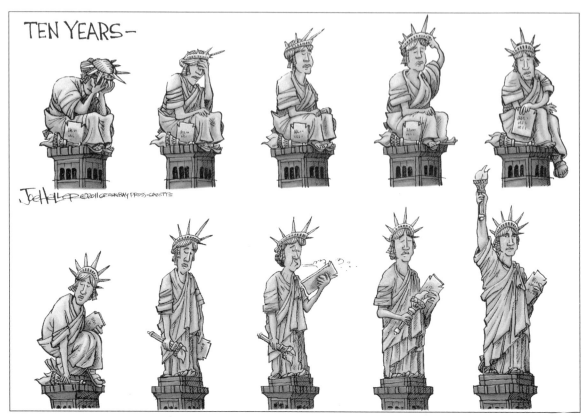

JOE HELLER
Courtesy Green Bay Press-Gazette

KEVIN SIERS
Courtesy Charlotte Observer

BOB GORRELL
Courtesy Gorrell Creative

GARY VARVEL
Courtesy Indianapolis Star

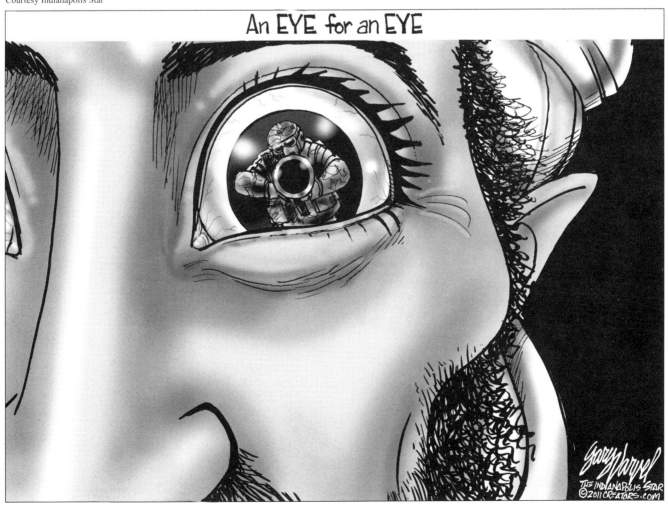

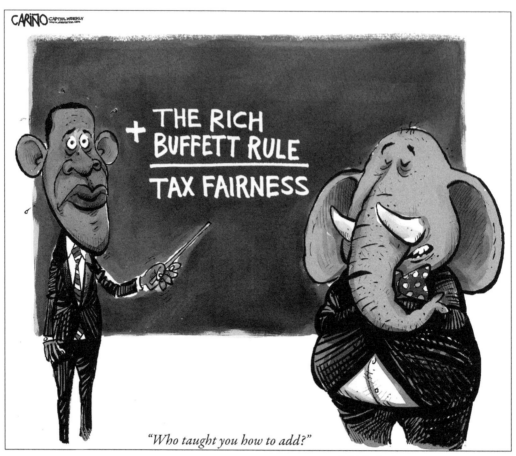

"Who taught you how to add?"

DAN CARINO
Courtesy THECARTOONMOVEMENT.COM

The Obama Administration

President Obama was challenged by a variety of problems—$4-a-gallon gas, high unemployment, an unstable stock market, and international unrest in the Arab world—in addition to U.S. military action in Afghanistan and Iraq.

With his approval sinking, Obama turned his attention to jobs. He demanded that millionaires pay more taxes. His proposal was dubbed the "Buffett Rule," for Warren Buffett, the billionaire investor who complained that rich people like him pay a smaller percentage of their income in federal taxes than do middle-class taxpayers.

Obama appealed for public support of his $447 billion proposal to boost jobs and consumer spending and urged Congress to "pass this bill right now." Obama's plan received a tepid reception from Republicans, who indicated a willingness to consider some of his tax relief proposals but not his spending plans.

Obama angered environmentalists by blocking EPA enforcement of stricter rules for air quality. He cited the recovering economy as the reason to abandon the regulations. He also approved construction of a 1,711-mile pipeline to bring oil from Canada to Texas.

The President finally produced a birth certificate, silencing at least some of those who doubted his American citizenship.

BOB GORRELL
Courtesy Gorrell Creative

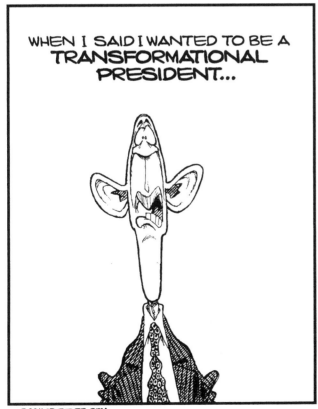

JEFF DARCY
Courtesy The Plain Dealer (Oh.)

GARY VARVEL
Courtesy Indianapolis Star

JAKE FULLER
Courtesy Artizans.com

STEVE BREEN
Courtesy San Diego Union-Tribune

31

RICK KOLLINGER
Courtesy Star-Democrat (Md.)

JERRY BREEN
Courtesy newbreen.com

STEVE LINDSTROM
Courtesy Duluth News-Tribune

32

JEFF DARCY
Courtesy The Plain Dealer (Oh.)

MICHAEL RAMIREZ
Courtesy Investors Business Daily

SCOTT STANTIS
Courtesy Chicago Tribune

NATE BEELER
Courtesy Washington Examiner

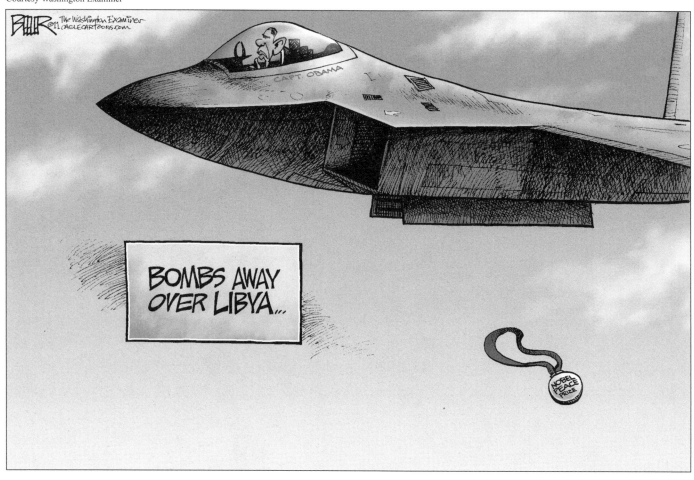

ED GAMBLE
Courtesy King Features Syndicate

ROB ROGERS
Courtesy Pittsburgh Post-Gazette

CHARLES BEYL
Courtesy Sunday News (Pa.)

JAKE FULLER
Courtesy Artizans.com

JERRY L. BARNETT
Courtesy Boonville Standard (Ind.)

MIKE GEMPELER
Courtesy Lee's Summit Journal

JAMES MORIN
Courtesy Miami Herald

ROBERT ARIAIL
Courtesy Spartanburg Herald-Journal

BOB GORRELL
Courtesy Gorrell Creative

RICHARD E. LOCHER
Courtesy Tribune Media Services

GARY VARVEL
Courtesy Indianapolis Star

39

GEORGE DANBY
Courtesy Bangor Daily News

JOHN RILEY
Courtesy John Riley

THOMAS BECK
Courtesy Freeport Journal-Standard (Ill.)

WALT HANDELSMAN
Courtesy Newsday

RICK MCKEE
Courtesy Augusta Chronicle

KEVIN SIERS
Courtesy Charlotte Observer

MICHAEL RAMIREZ
Courtesy Investors Business Daily

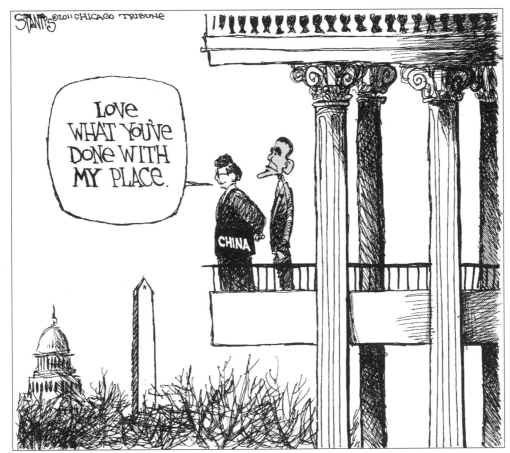

SCOTT STANTIS
Courtesy Chicago Tribune

WILLIAM WARREN
Courtesy Liberty Features Syndicate

43

TIM BENSON
Courtesy The Argus-Leader

44

The Debt Crisis

A major battle took shape in Congress over raising the national debt ceiling. House Republicans fought against increasing the $14 trillion debt limitation without drastic cuts in spending. Republican Cong. Paul Ryan presented a bold plan to reduce the deficit, but the plan was roundly criticized by Democrats and even some Republicans for its proposed drastic budget cuts.

The House passed a bill to cut and cap spending and pass a balanced budget amendment, but Senate Democrats refused to consider it. Instead, Democrats sought to reduce the nation's deficit through a combination of spending cuts and tax increases. Republicans balked at raising taxes as part of any deficit reduction. As the deadline for a threatened government default neared, an eleventh-hour deal was struck to raise the nation's debt limit from $14 trillion to more than $16 trillion. The agreement aimed to cut the federal budget deficit by $2.5 trillion over the next decade.

The financial rating agency Standard & Poor's downgraded the U.S. credit rating from AAA to AA. Democrats blamed Tea Party Republicans for the downgrade, asserting their intransigence made creditors doubt that the U.S. was a safe place to invest. The whole debt mess tarred both parties, sinking Congress's public approval even further.

CHRIS WEYANT
Courtesy The Hill

TIM BENSON
Courtesy The Argus-Leader

MARK STREETER
Courtesy Savannah Morning News

BOB GORRELL
Courtesy Gorrell Creative

DAVID HORSEY
Courtesy Hearst Newspapers

47

DAN CARINO
Courtesy THECARTOONMOVEMENT.COM

ADAM ZYGLIS
Courtesy Buffalo News

RICK MCKEE
Courtesy Augusta Chronicle

JEFF PARKER
Courtesy Florida Today

GRAEME MACKAY
Courtesy Hamilton Spectator (Ont.)

RICK MCKEE
Courtesy Augusta Chronicle

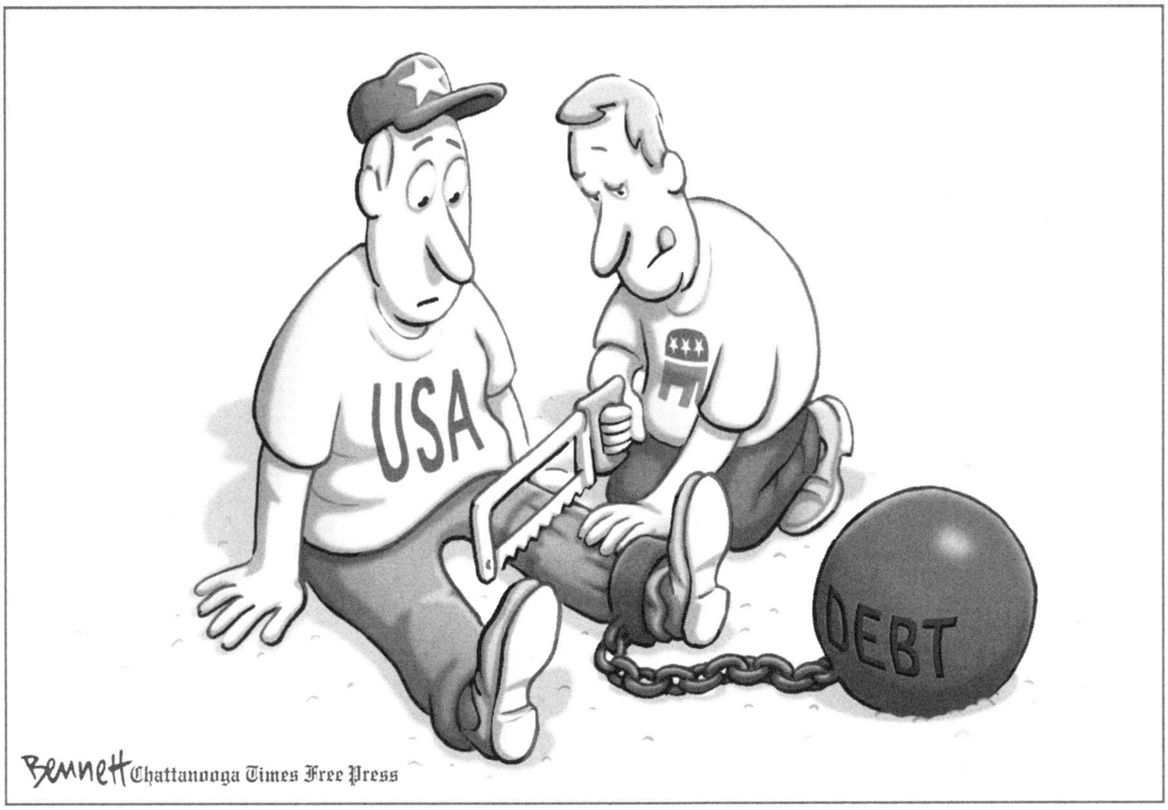
USA
DEBT
Bennett Chattanooga Times Free Press

CLAY BENNETT
Courtesy Chattanooga Times-Free Press

SCOTT STANTIS
Courtesy Chicago Tribune

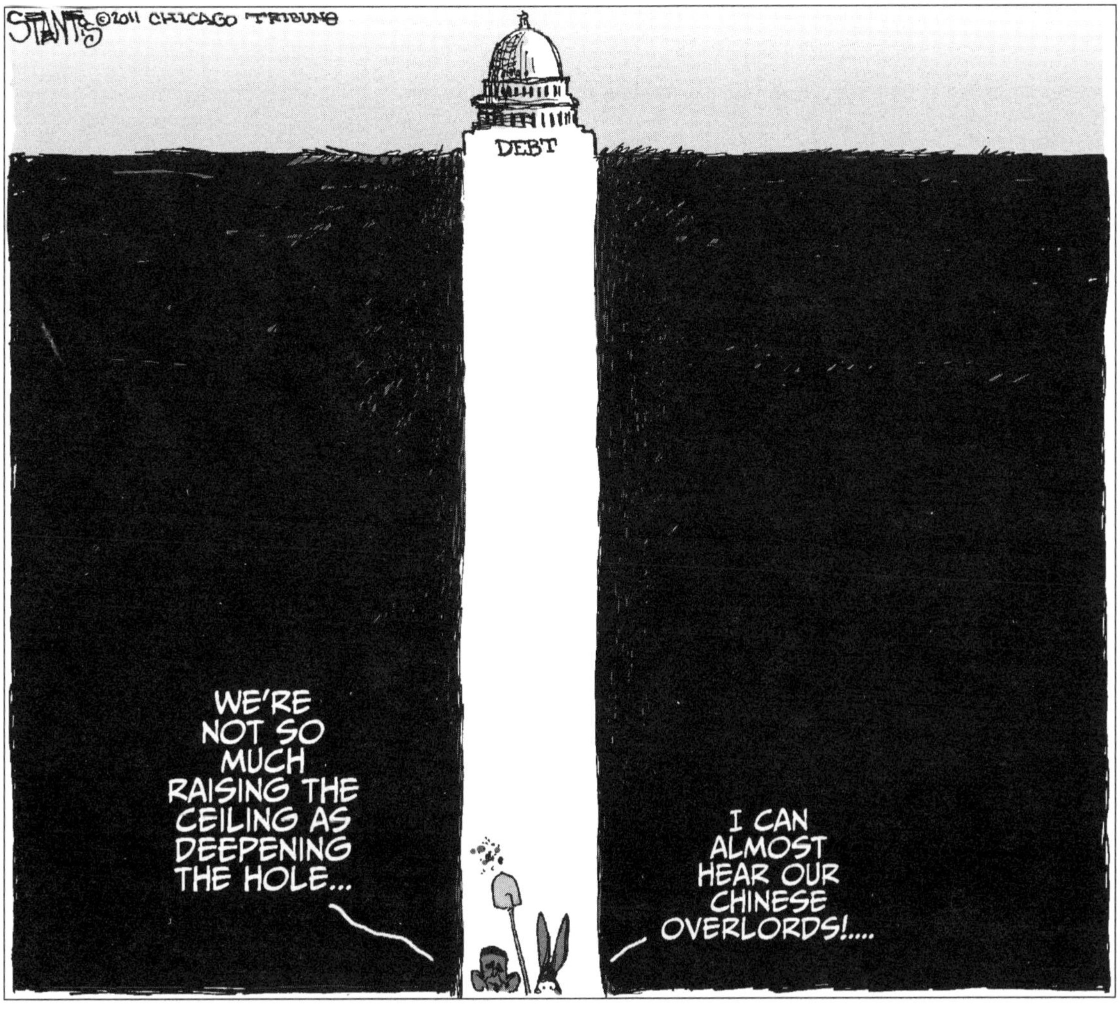
STANTIS ©2011 CHICAGO TRIBUNE
DEBT
WE'RE NOT SO MUCH RAISING THE CEILING AS DEEPENING THE HOLE...
I CAN ALMOST HEAR OUR CHINESE OVERLORDS!....

JOHN BRANCH
Courtesy Branchtoon.com/
    North American Syndicate

TIMOTHY JACKSON
Courtesy Chicago Defender

DAVID DONAR
Courtesy donarfilms

CHAN LOWE
Courtesy Tribune Media

RICHARD E. LOCHER
Courtesy Tribune Media Services

PETER EVANS
Courtesy The Islander News (Fla.)

MICHAEL POHRER
Courtesy National Free Press

JERRY L. BARNETT
Courtesy Boonville Standard (Ind.)

REPUBLICANS and DEMOCRATS TO SOON FIND COMMON GROUND...

STEVE BREEN
Courtesy San Diego Union-Tribune

RICK MCKEE
Courtesy Augusta Chronicle

MIKE MARLAND
Courtesy Concord Monitor

ROBERT ARIAIL
Courtesy Spartanburg Herald-Journal

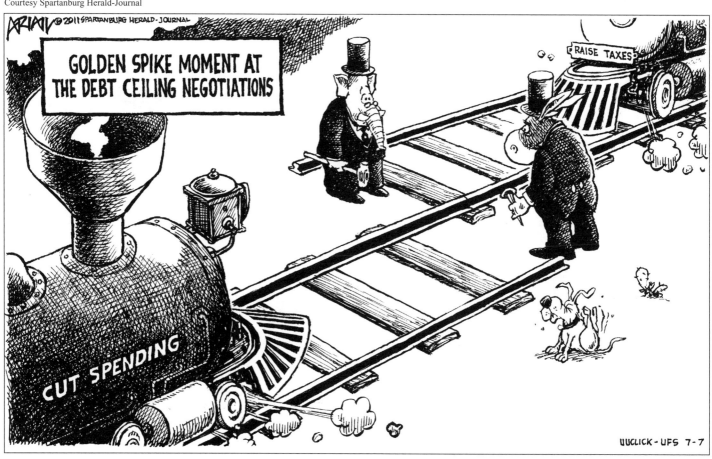

STEVE KELLEY
Courtesy The Times-Picayune (La.)

LISA BENSON
Courtesy Washington Post Writers Group

ASSAD

Drip off the old block

JOHN SHERFFIUS
Courtesy Boulder Camera

NATE BEELER
Courtesy Washington Examiner

NEWS ITEM: PRO-ASSAD THUGS TRY TO SILENCE SYRIAN CARTOONIST BY BREAKING HIS HANDS

Foreign Affairs

Civil uprisings spread across the Arab world in a movement that became known as the Arab Spring. Citizens took the streets in Cairo, toppling Egyptian President Hosni Mubarak. In Syria, however, the government refused to go quietly, sending tanks and troops against civilians, killing thousands. NATO, led by European nations and the U.S., lent air support to Libyan rebels who overthrew the regime of Moammar Gadhafi and killed the dictator in the street.

President Obama came under fire for allowing France to take the lead in ousting the Libyan leader. The months-long bitter fighting ended with the rebels taking Gadhafi's stronghold in Tripoli. Revolutionary demonstrations and protests occurred in many other Arab countries. Protesters made use of modern technology, including social media. Palestinian leader Mahmoud Abbas applied to the U.N. for statehood.

Violence erupted in Greece over budget-cutting measures, and an earthquake and tsunami devastated the northeast coast of Japan, crippling a nuclear power plant. Famine relief reached 1.85 million Somalis, but tens of thousands died.

In Norway, a radical opposed to Muslim immigration bombed a government office in Oslo, then opened fire on a youth gathering, killing 91.

MIKE PETERS
Courtesy Dayton Daily News

59

GUY BADEAUX
Courtesy Le Droit (Can.)

STEVE BREEN
Courtesy San Diego Union-Tribune

JOEL PETT
Courtesy Lexington Herald-Leader

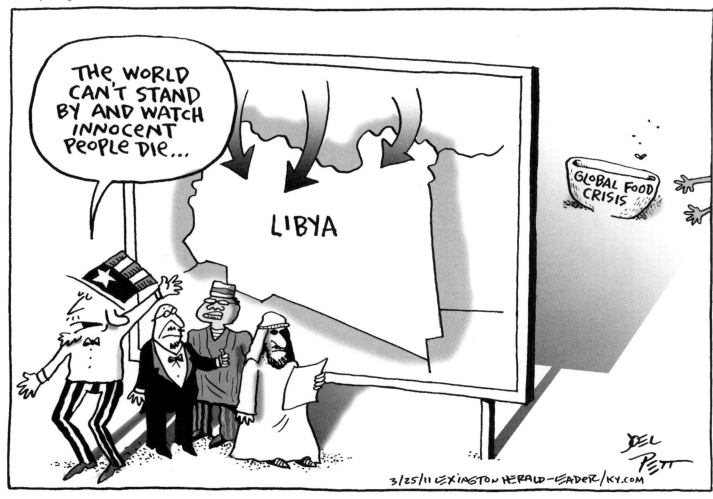

KEVIN SIERS
Courtesy Charlotte Observer

GRAEME MACKAY
Courtesy Hamilton Spectator (Ont.)

61

TIM BENSON
Courtesy The Argus-Leader

JEFF DANZIGER
Courtesy NYTS/CWS

ROBERT ARIAIL
Courtesy Spartanburg Herald-Journal

62

BOB LANG
Courtesy Rightoons.com

JOHN BRANCH
Courtesy Branchtoon.com/
    North American Syndicate

KEVIN KALLAUGHER
Courtesy The Economist

JAMES MORIN
Courtesy Miami Herald

STEVE GREENBERG
Courtesy Ventura County Reporter (Calif.)

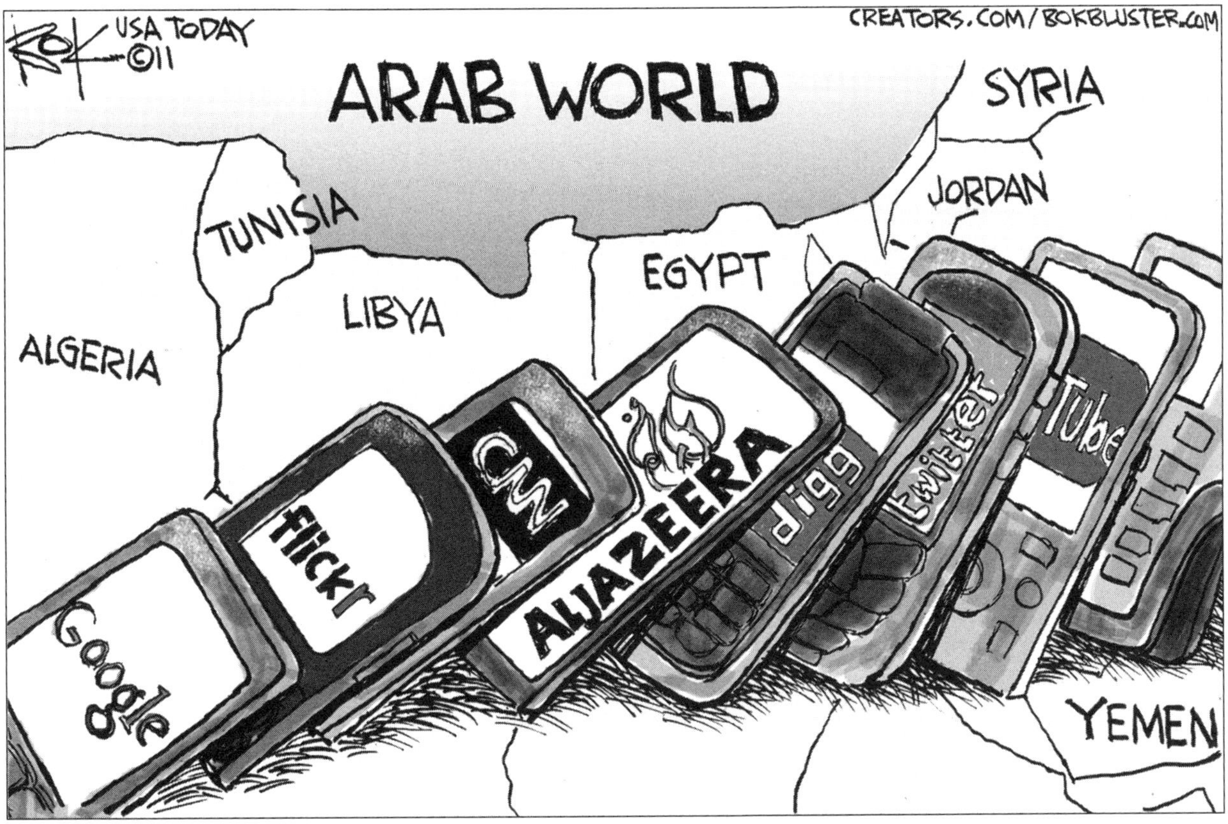
BOK USA TODAY ©11
CREATORS.COM/BOKBLUSTER.COM
ARAB WORLD
SYRIA
JORDAN
TUNISIA
EGYPT
LIBYA
ALGERIA
Google
flickr
CNN
ALJAZEERA
digg
twitter
Tube
YEMEN

CHIP BOK
Courtesy Creators Syndicate

J.D. CROWE
Courtesy Mobile Press-Register

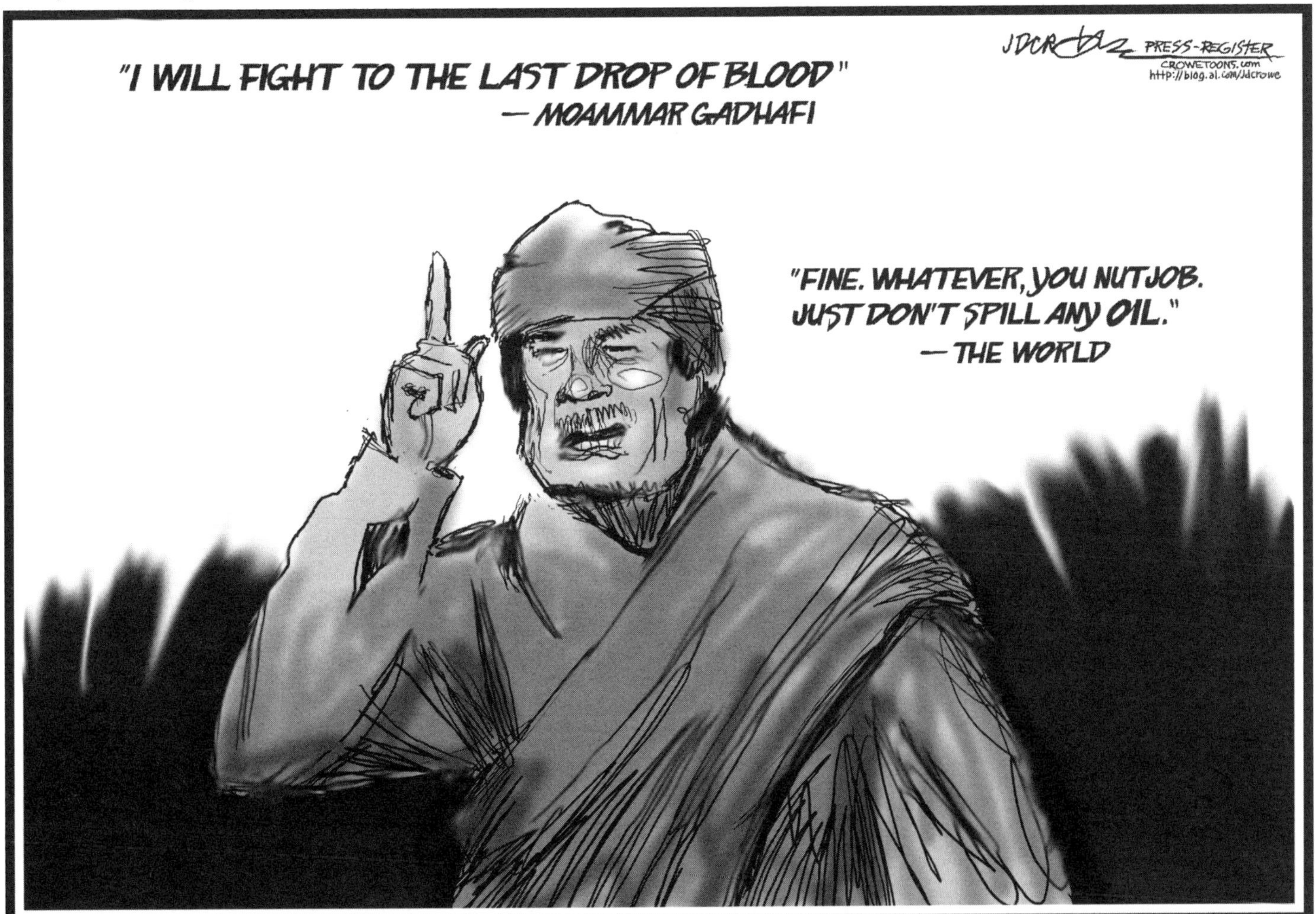
JDCROWE PRESS-REGISTER
CROWETOONS.com
http://blog.al.com/jdcrowe
"I WILL FIGHT TO THE LAST DROP OF BLOOD"
— MOAMMAR GADHAFI
"FINE. WHATEVER, YOU NUTJOB. JUST DON'T SPILL ANY OIL."
— THE WORLD

MUBARAK

MIKE PETERS
Courtesy Dayton Daily News

JOHN SHERFFIUS
Courtesy Boulder Camera

Boulder Camera © 1/31/11creators.com
jsherffius@gmail.com
sherffius.com

DAVID HORSEY
Courtesy Hearst Newspapers

ROBERT ARIAIL
Courtesy Spartanburg Herald-Journal

GEOFFREY MOSS
Courtesy Creators Syndicate

GRAEME MACKAY
Courtesy Hamilton Spectator (Ont.)

STEVE MCBRIDE
Courtesy The Reporter

LISA BENSON
Courtesy Washington Post Writers Group

MIKE LUCKOVICH
Courtesy Atlanta Journal-Constitution

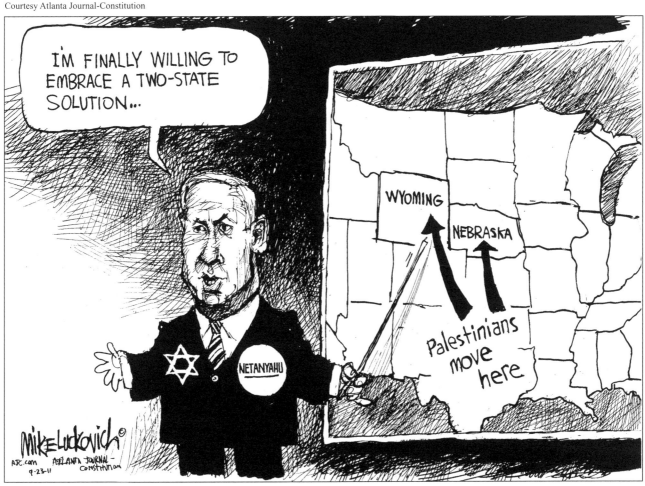

DAVID HITCH
Courtesy Telegram & Gazette (Mass.)

GRAEME MACKAY
Courtesy Hamilton Spectator (Ont.)

MIKE BECKOM
Courtesy beckomtoonz@aol.com

CLAY BENNETT
Courtesy Chattanooga Times-Free Press

DAN CARINO
Courtesy THECARTOONMOVEMENT.COM

BARRY HUNAU
Courtesy Jerusalem Post

JEFF HICKMAN
Courtesy Reno Gazette-Journal

KEVIN KALLAUGHER
Courtesy The Economist

STEVE KELLEY
Courtesy The Times-Picayune (La.)

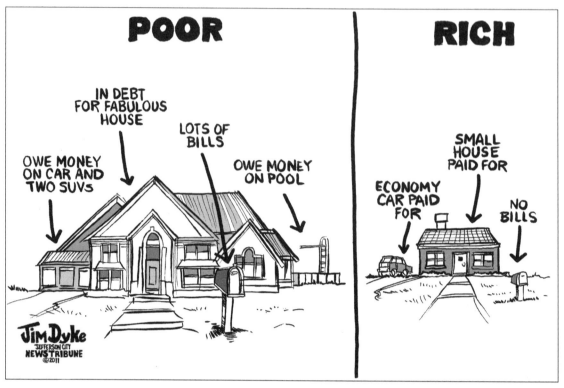

JIM DYKE
Courtesy Jefferson City News-Tribune

CHIP BOK
Courtesy Creators Syndicate

The Economy

The economy dominated the news in 2011. The stock market took a wild roller coaster ride, unemployment remained stuck at more than 9 percent, and the housing market remained in a slump. President Obama's stimulus spending, designed to create jobs, instead drowned the budget in red ink.

Economists warned that the nation's burdensome debt could lead the U.S. down the same path of violent protests that have plagued Greece, which is teetering on default. Most of the European Union is also drowning in debt, decreasing the value of the euro. Bank failures continued unabated, and China held a large portion of America's debt. The credit rating agency Standard & Poor's downgraded the U.S. from AAA to AA after a contentious battle in Congress over the debt ceiling.

The Republican-dominated House and Democrat-dominated Senate were unable to reach agreement to help get the economy of its slump. Soaring gas prices put an additional bite on Americans.

A New York Times/CBS News poll showed nearly half of those surveyed worried about another recession. Nearly three out of four said they believe the country is on the wrong track. The sluggish economy was seen as a serious threat to President Obama's chances to win reelection.

"Buy American" was not a good slogan for the Canadian economy.

STEVE KELLEY
Courtesy The Times-Picayune (La.)

GEORGE DANBY
Courtesy Bangor Daily News

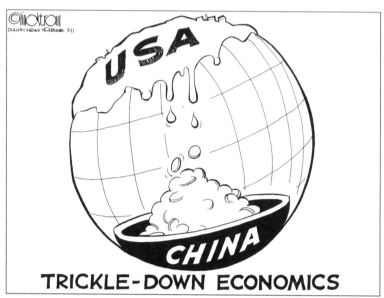

STEVE LINDSTROM
Courtesy Duluth News-Tribune

JERRY L. BARNETT
Courtesy Boonville Standard (Ind.)

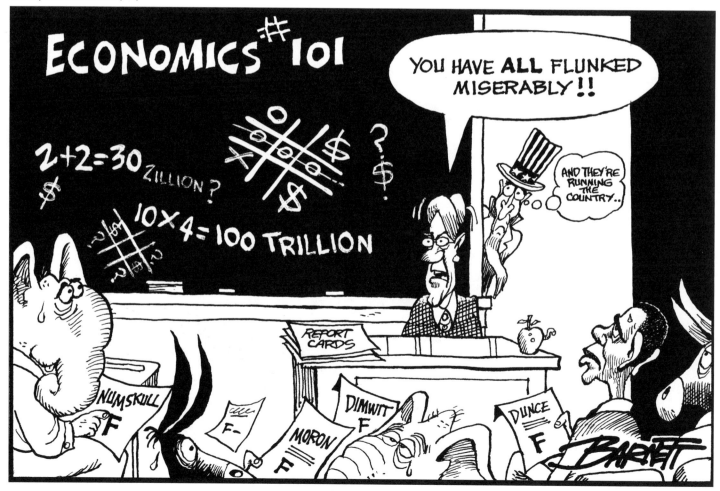

RICHARD E. LOCHER
Courtesy Tribune Media Services

WALT HANDELSMAN
Courtesy Newsday

STEVE MCBRIDE
Courtesy The Reporter

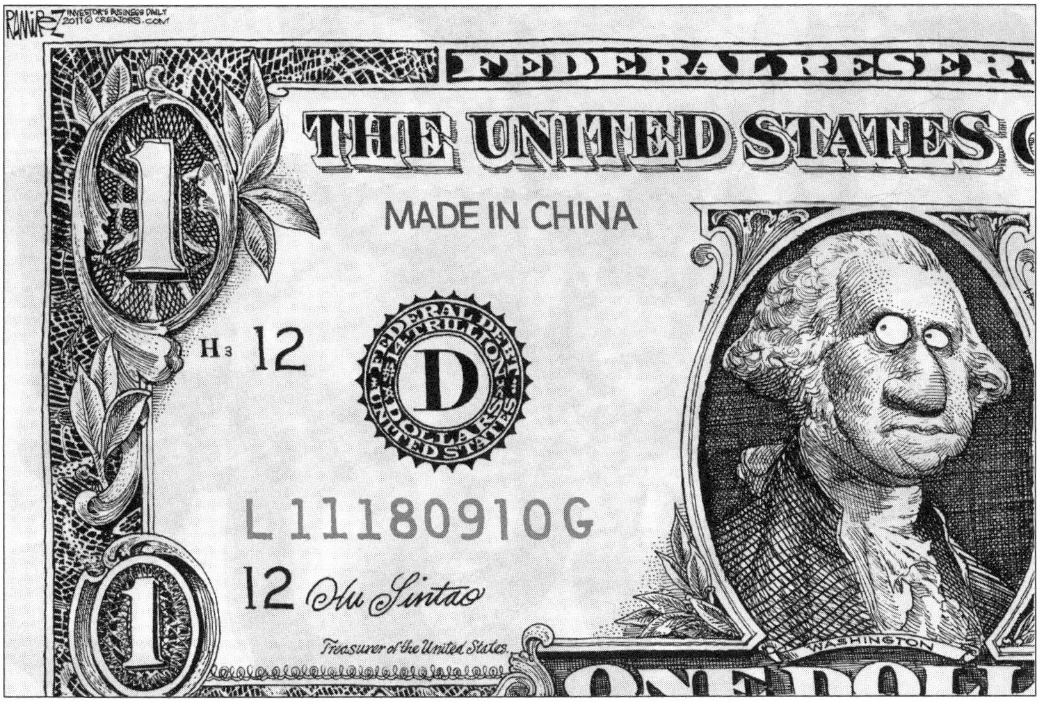
RAMIREZ INVESTOR'S BUSINESS DAILY 2011© CREATORS.COM
FEDERAL RESERV
THE UNITED STATES
MADE IN CHINA
H3 12
FEDERAL DEBT 14 TRILLION DOLLARS UNITED STATES
D
L11180910G
12 Hu Jintao
Treasurer of the United States
WASHINGTON
ONE DOLL

MICHAEL RAMIREZ
Courtesy Investors Business Daily

TAYLOR JONES
Courtesy cagletoons.com

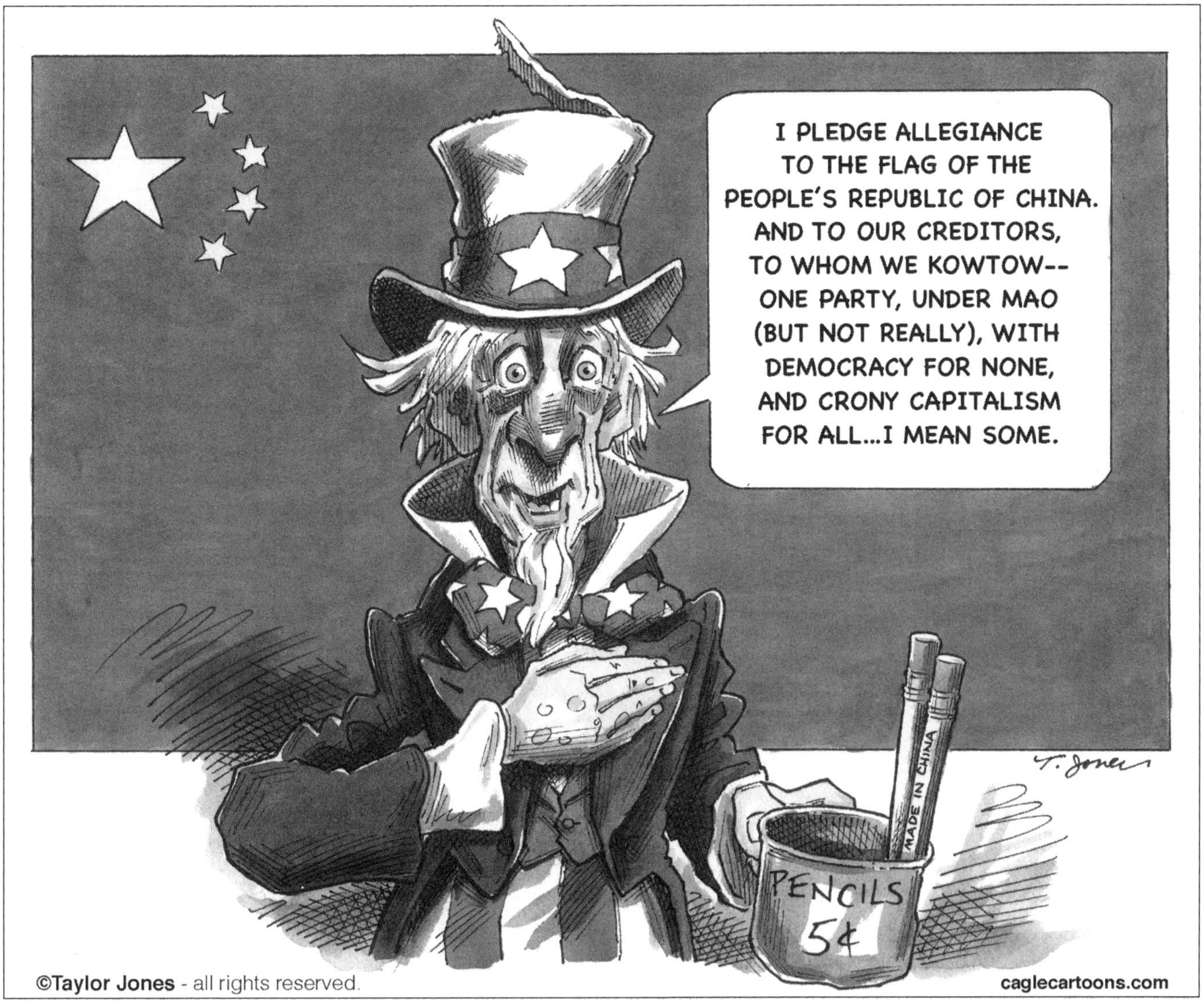
I PLEDGE ALLEGIANCE TO THE FLAG OF THE PEOPLE'S REPUBLIC OF CHINA. AND TO OUR CREDITORS, TO WHOM WE KOWTOW-- ONE PARTY, UNDER MAO (BUT NOT REALLY), WITH DEMOCRACY FOR NONE, AND CRONY CAPITALISM FOR ALL...I MEAN SOME.
T. Jones
MADE IN CHINA
PENCILS 5¢
©Taylor Jones - all rights reserved.
caglecartoons.com

LISA BENSON
Courtesy Washington Post Writers Group

JOE LICCAR
Courtesy The Examiner (Mo.)

JESSE SPRINGER
Courtesy Eugene Register-Guard

80

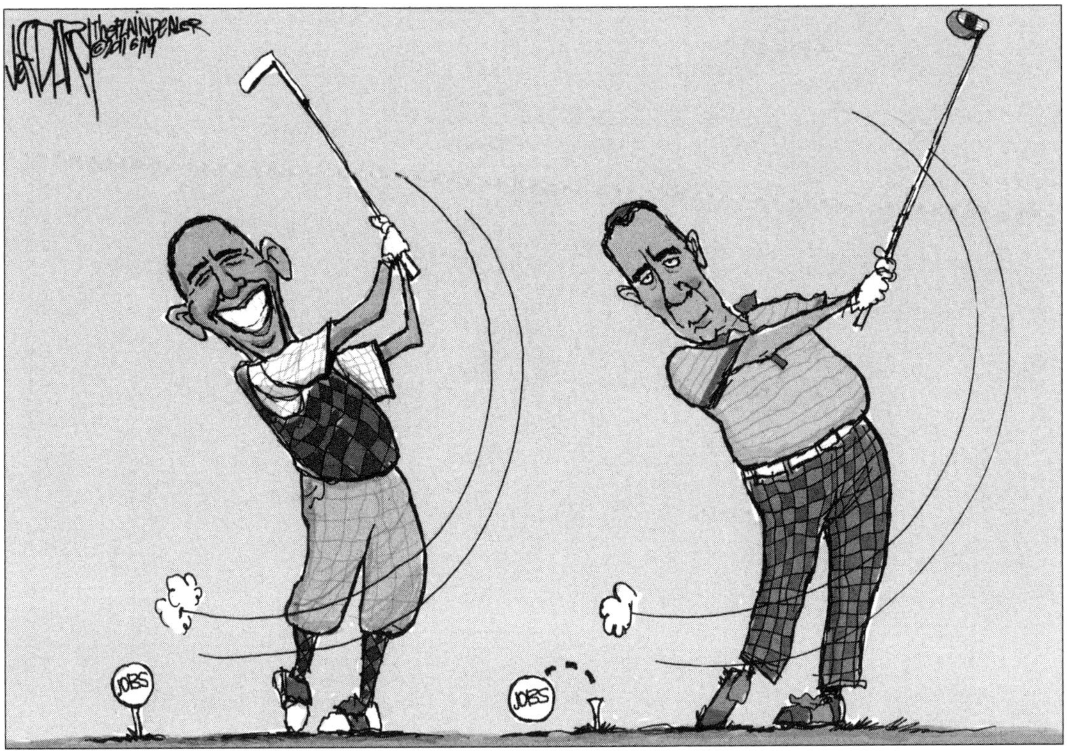
JOBS
JOBS

JEFF DARCY
Courtesy The Plain Dealer (Oh.)

POL GALVEZ
Courtesy Philippine News (Calif.)

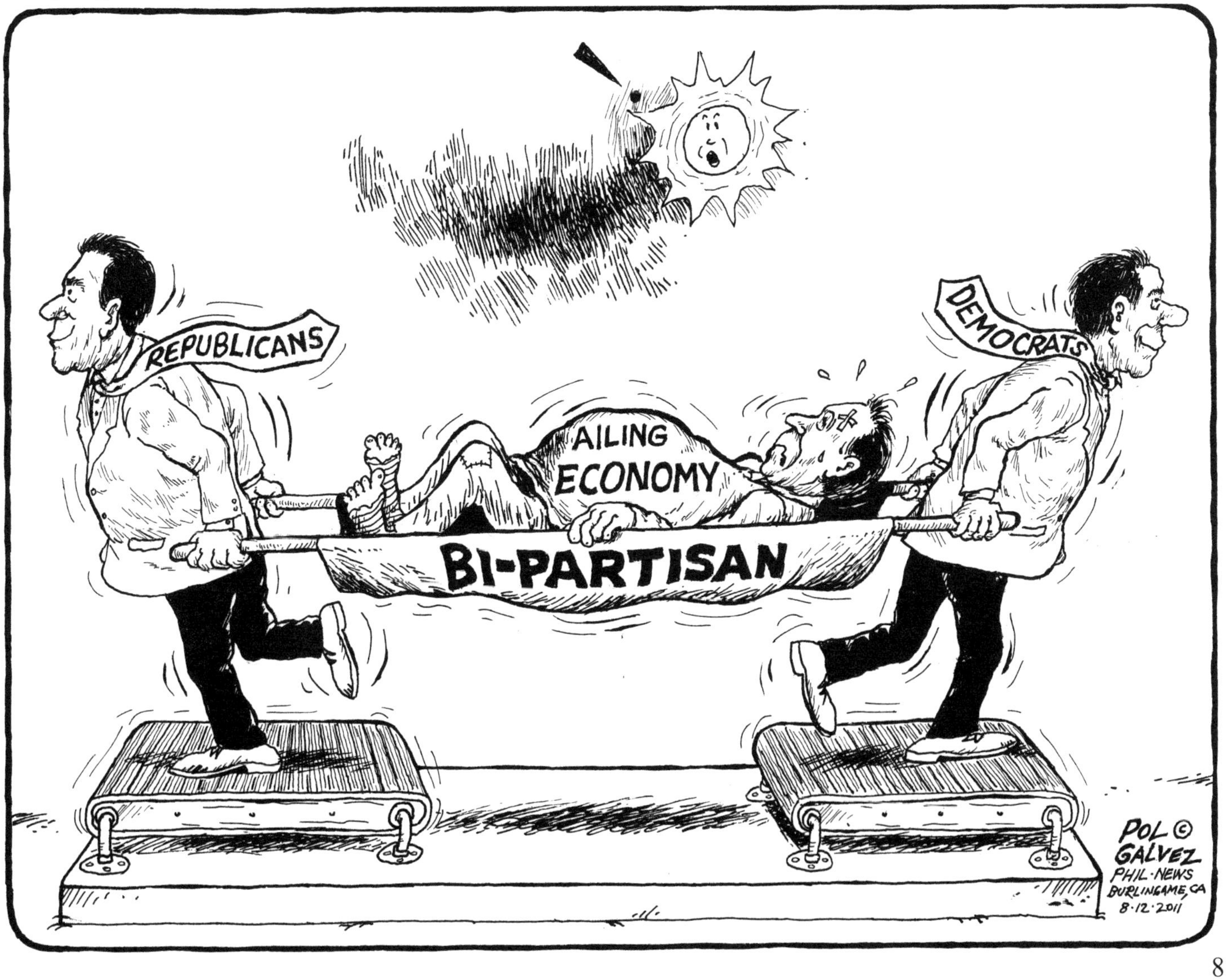
REPUBLICANS
DEMOCRATS
AILING ECONOMY
BI-PARTISAN
POL © GALVEZ PHIL·NEWS BURLINGAME, CA 8·12·2011

ANN CLEAVES
Courtesy Ann Cleaves

KARL WIMER
Courtesy Denver Business Journal

ED GAMBLE
Courtesy King Features Syndicate

STEVE BREEN
Courtesy San Diego Union-Tribune

GUY BADEAUX
Courtesy Le Droit (Can.)

STEVE NEASE
Courtesy Nease Cartoons

JUSTIN DEFREITAS
Courtesy East Bay Express (Calif.)

PETER EVANS
Courtesy The Islander News (Fla.)

TIM DOLIGHAN
Courtesy Dolighan Cartoons

JEFF PARKER
Courtesy Florida Today

BOB LANG
Courtesy Rightoons.com

JERRY L. BARNETT
Courtesy Boonville Standard (Ind.)

JIM SIERGEY
Courtesy jimsiergey.com

JOSEPH O'MAHONEY
Courtesy The Patriot Ledger

GUY BADEAUX
Courtesy Le Droit (Can.)

ELIZABETH BRICQUET
Courtesy Kingsport Times-News

ROBERT ENGLEHART
Courtesy Hartford Courant

Politics

Republican candidates jockeyed for position to challenge President Obama in 2012. The early favorite was former Massachusetts Gov. Mitt Romney, followed closely by Minnesota Rep. Michele Bachmann and Texas Rep. Ron Paul. Former Minnesota Gov. Tim Pawlenty was an early casualty.

Former Texas Gov. Rick Perry entered the race soon afterward, and immediately shot to the top rank, posing a formidable challenge to Romney. He later seemed to falter. Former Godfather's Pizza CEO Herman Cain emerged as a serious contender. Sarah Palin, who made a few gaffes, announced in October she would not be a candidate, and Newt Gingrich came under fire for running a lackadaisical campaign. Many of his staff resigned.

Approval ratings for Congress and President Obama plunged to record lows along with the economy. Democrats attacked Tea Party members for their unwillingness to compromise on the debt ceiling. In what could be bad news for President Obama in 2012, GOP political novice Bob Turner defeated Democrat assemblyman David Weprin in a heavily Democratic district to fill the seat vacated by Rep. Anthony Weiner, who resigned in disgrace after an online sex scandal.

Former California Gov. Arnold Schwarzenegger admitted fathering a child with the family housekeeper.

THEO MOUDAKIS
Courtesy Toronto Star

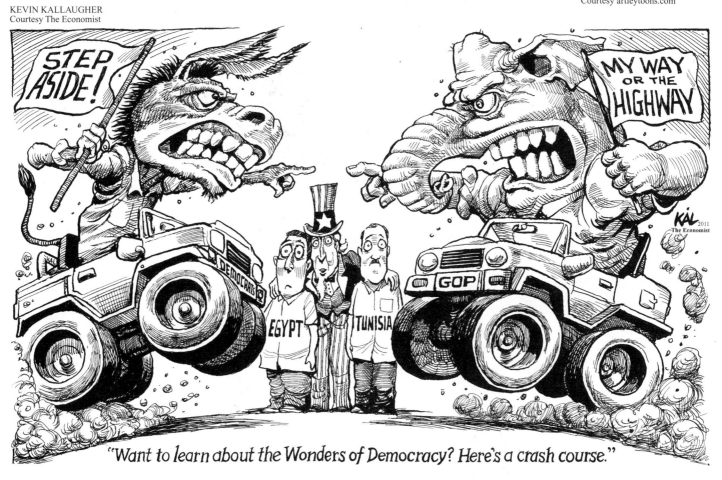

"Want to learn about the Wonders of Democracy? Here's a crash course."

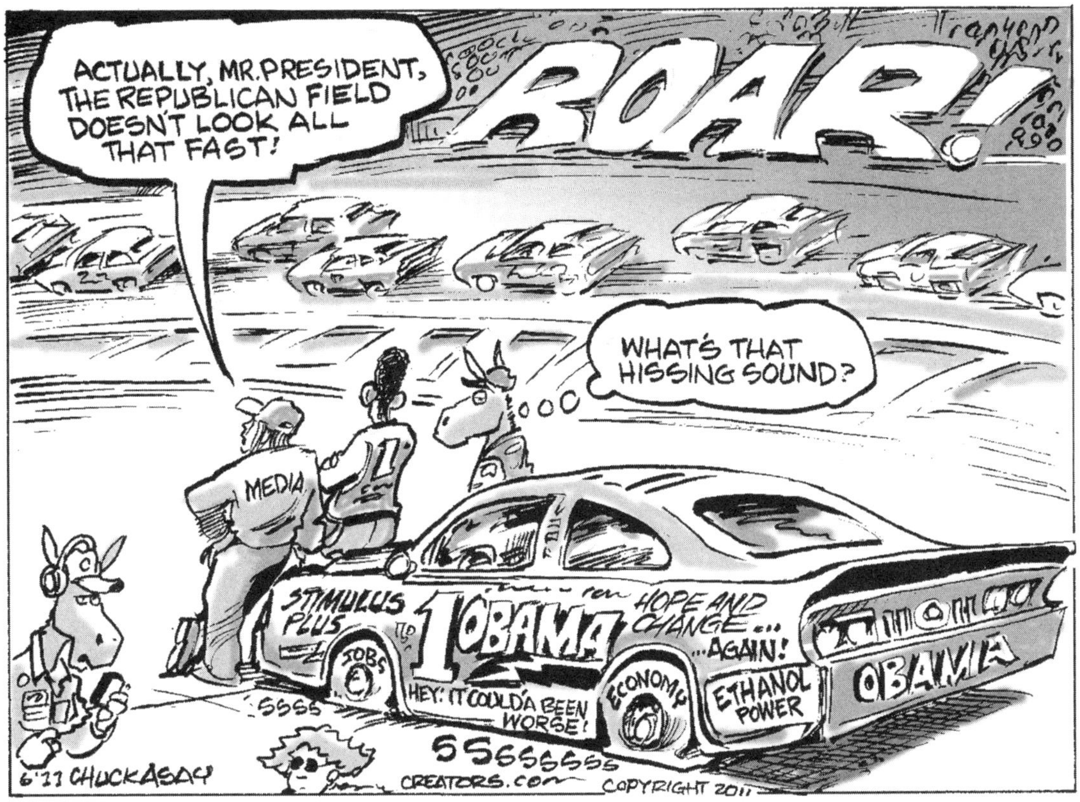
ACTUALLY, MR. PRESIDENT, THE REPUBLICAN FIELD DOESN'T LOOK ALL THAT FAST!
ROAR!
WHAT'S THAT HISSING SOUND?
MEDIA
STIMULUS PLUS
1 OBAMA
HOPE AND CHANGE... ...AGAIN!
JOBS
HEY: IT COULD'A BEEN WORSE!
ECONOMY
ETHANOL POWER
OBAMA
SSSS
SSSSSSSSS
6'23 CHUCKASAY
CREATORS.COM
COPYRIGHT 2011

CHUCK ASAY
Courtesy Creators.com

MIKE PETERS
Courtesy Dayton Daily News

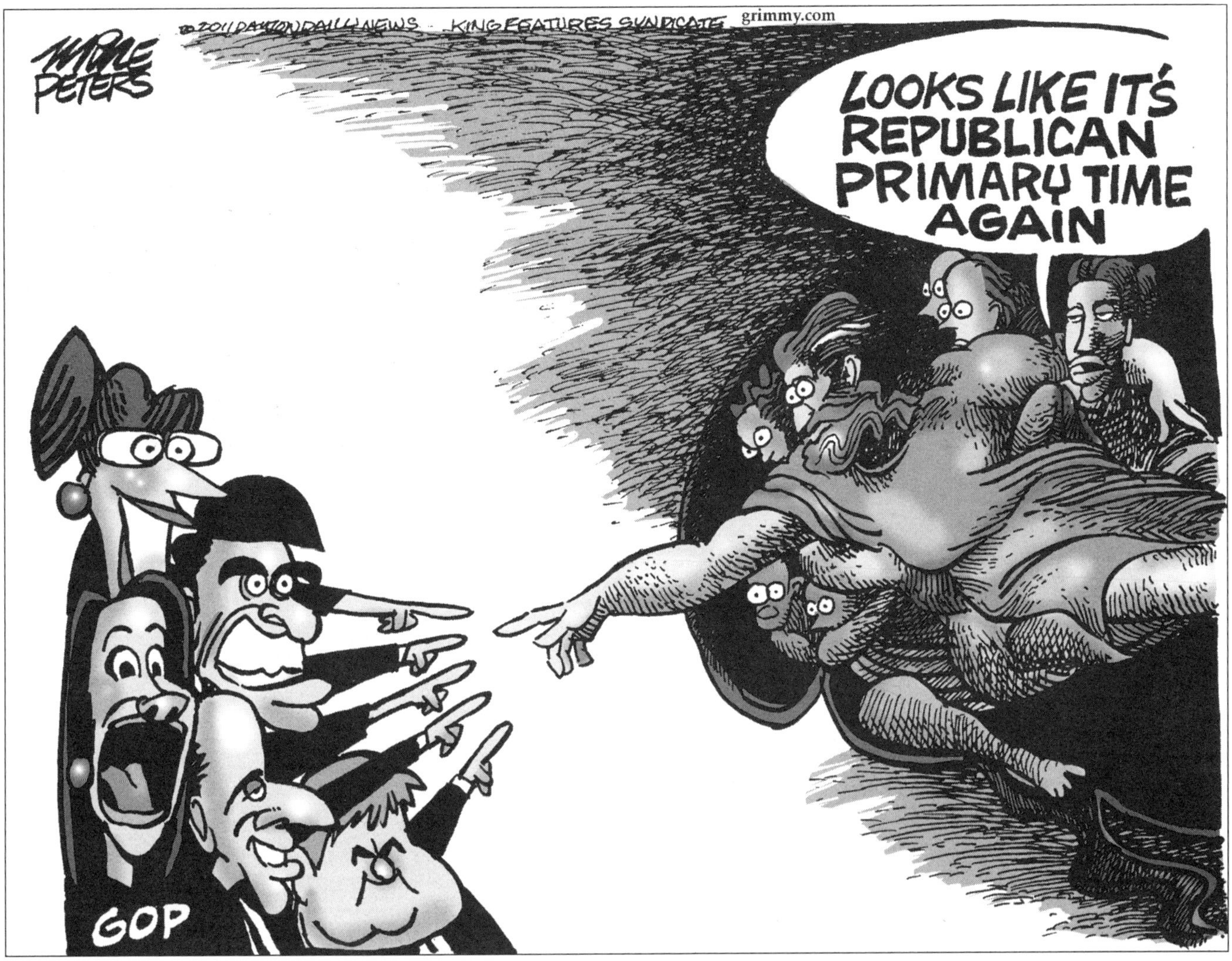
grimmy.com
MIKE PETERS
LOOKS LIKE IT'S REPUBLICAN PRIMARY TIME AGAIN
GOP

JOHN BRANCH
Courtesy Branchtoon.com/
North American Syndicate

ED STEIN
Courtesy EDSTEININK.COM

ED GAMBLE
Courtesy King Features Syndicate

MIKE PETERS
Courtesy Dayton Daily News

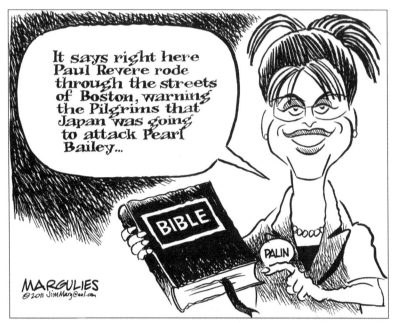

JIMMY MARGULIES
Courtesy North Jersey Media Group

JERRY BREEN
Courtesy newbreen.com

JEFF HICKMAN
Courtesy Reno Gazette-Journal

BRUCE PLANTE
Courtesy Tulsa World

MIKE GEMPELER
Courtesy Lee's Summit Journal

TIM DOLIGHAN
Courtesy Dolighan Cartoons

JEFF STAHLER
Courtesy Columbus Dispatch

MARC MURPHY
Courtesy Louisville Courier-Journal

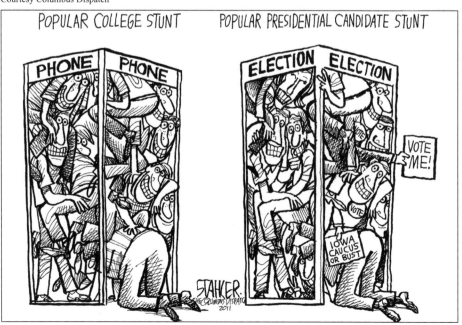

The Tea Party

CLAY BENNETT
Courtesy Chattanooga Times-Free Press

KEVIN KALLAUGHER
Courtesy The Economist

STEVE LINDSTROM
Courtesy Duluth News-Tribune

MIKE SPICER
Courtesy Mike's Cartoons

THOMAS BECK
Courtesy Freeport Journal-Standard (Ill.)

PHIL HANDS
Courtesy Wisconsin State Journal

MIKE LUCKOVICH
Courtesy Atlanta Journal-Constitution

CLAY BENNETT
Courtesy Chattanooga Times-Free Press

HAP PITKIN
Courtesy Boulder Camera

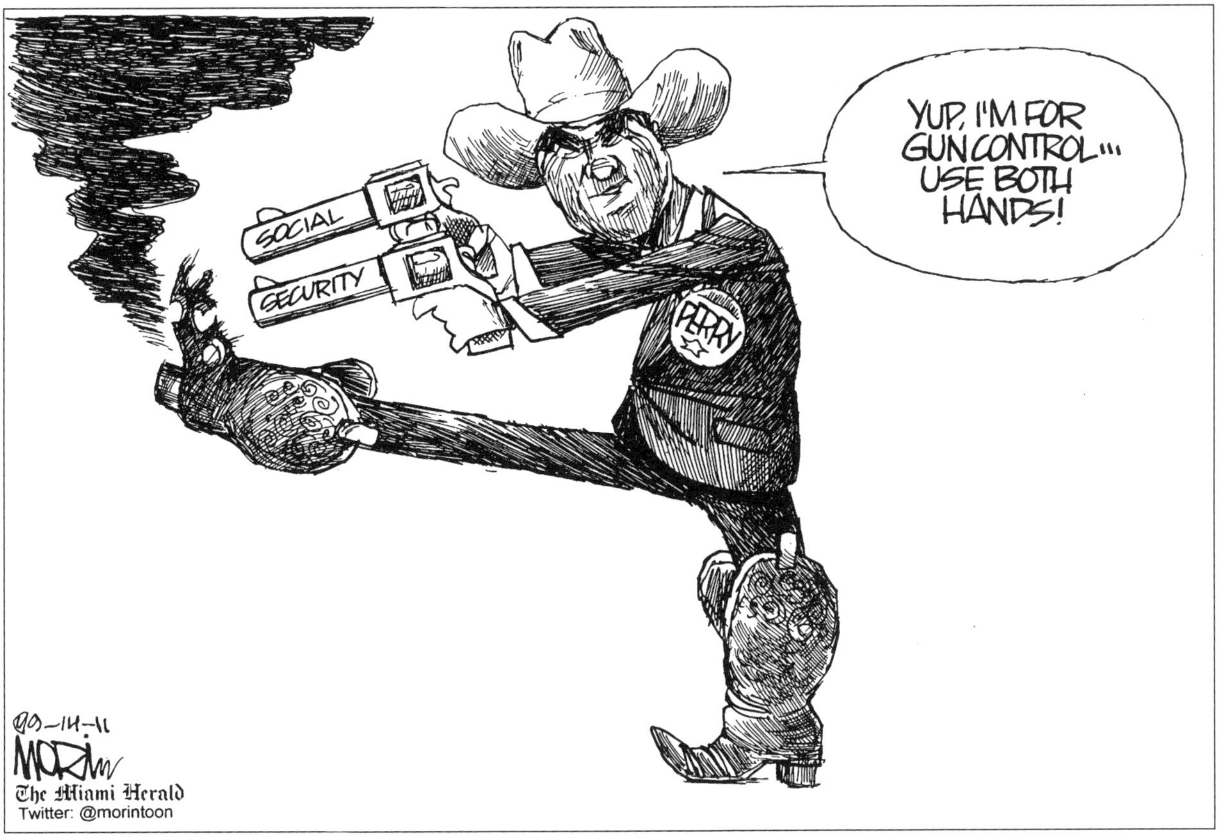
YUP, I'M FOR GUN CONTROL... USE BOTH HANDS!
SOCIAL
SECURITY
PERRY
09-14-11
MORIN
The Miami Herald
Twitter: @morintoon

JAMES MORIN
Courtesy Miami Herald

TAYLOR JONES
Courtesy cagletoons.com

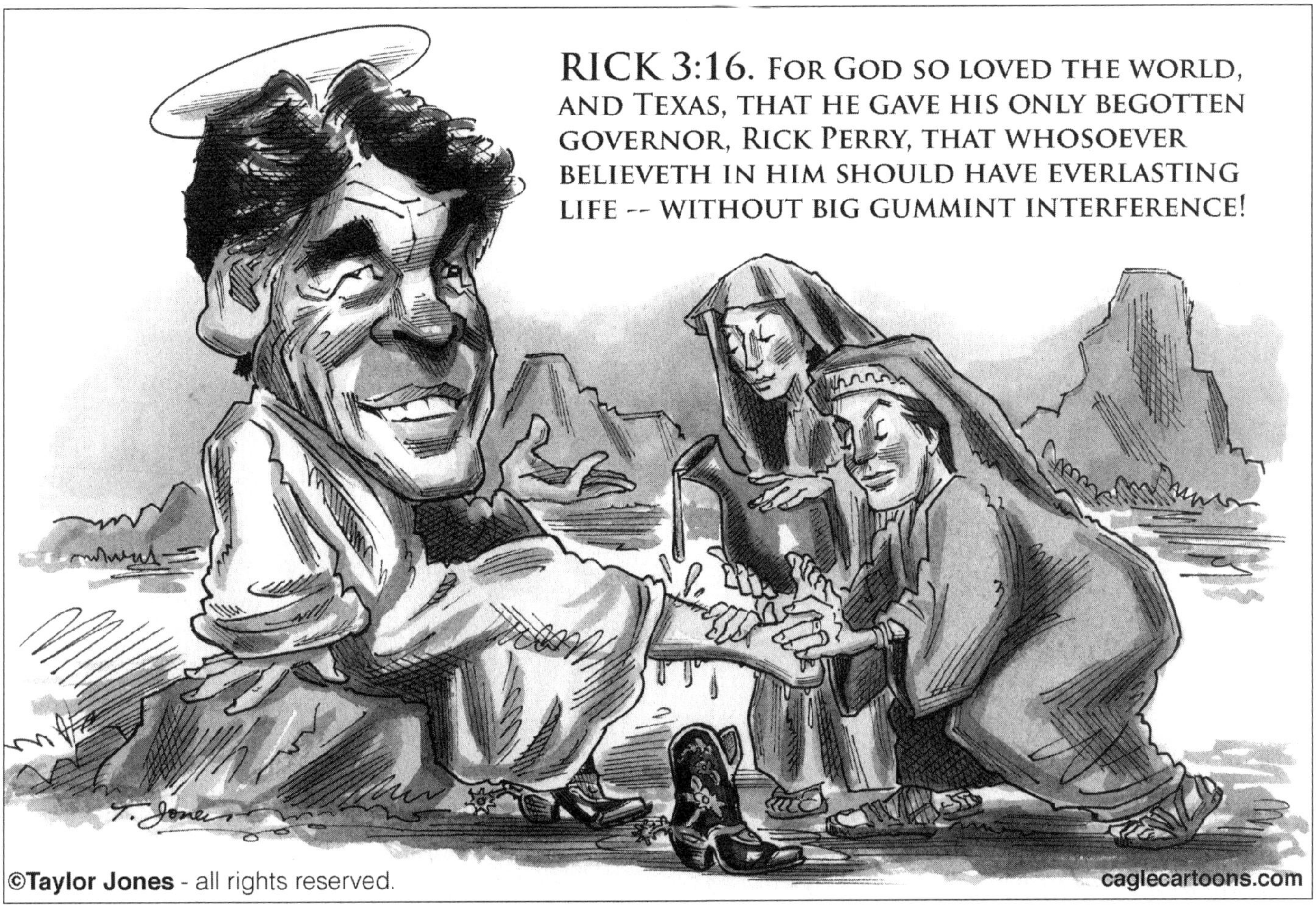
RICK 3:16. FOR GOD SO LOVED THE WORLD, AND TEXAS, THAT HE GAVE HIS ONLY BEGOTTEN GOVERNOR, RICK PERRY, THAT WHOSOEVER BELIEVETH IN HIM SHOULD HAVE EVERLASTING LIFE -- WITHOUT BIG GUMMINT INTERFERENCE!
T. Jones
©Taylor Jones - all rights reserved.
caglecartoons.com

STEVE LINDSTROM
Courtesy Duluth News-Tribune

DICK WALLMEYER
Courtesy Long Beach Press-Telegram

CHRIS BRITT
Courtesy State Journal-Register (Ill.)

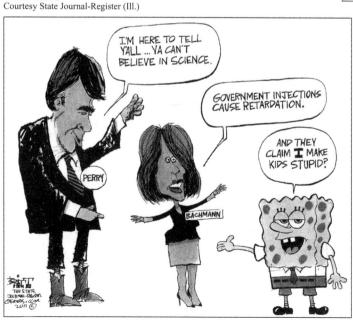

Unconventional Republican Mavericks

ROB ROGERS
Courtesy Pittsburgh Post-Gazette

MILT PRIGGEE
Courtesy miltpriggee.com

BRUCE PLANTE
Courtesy Tulsa World

MIKE LUCKOVICH
Courtesy Atlanta Journal-Constitution

WARNING LABELS WE WOULDN'T MIND SEEING

| CIGARETTES | FATTY FOODS | POLITICIANS |

TIM HARTMAN
Courtesy Beaver County Times-Record (Pa.)

ADAM ZYGLIS
Courtesy Buffalo News

105

MIKE PETERS
Courtesy Dayton Daily News

Congress

Congress's rating plummeted to new lows following a partisan battle over raising the debt ceiling. The partisan brinksmanship almost led to a government shutdown. Polls showed voters were disenchanted with both parties.

After the debt-ceiling debacle, a 12-member bipartisan "super-committee" was formed to deal with the debt crisis. Republicans wanted deep cuts to balance the nation's budget, but balked at raising taxes, as Democrats demanded. President Obama brought his jobs proposal to the "super-committee." Tea Party Republicans wanted a return to a strict interpretation of the U.S. Constitution as written by the founders. Democrats demanded even more spending.

On the heels of Hurricane Irene and Texas wildfires, House Majority Leader Eric Cantor proposed that any new disaster relief funds be offset by cuts elsewhere in the federal budget. After an earthquake in his state of Virginia, however, Cantor sought disaster relief funds for his district.

Rep. Anthony Weiner resigned after admitting he sent a photo of his crotch on Twitter to a student. At first he denied that he did so, but finally admitted to "inappropriate relationships" with six women. Rep. Gabrielle Giffords returned to Congress for a vote after being shot at an open meeting in Arizona.

MICHAEL RAMIREZ
Courtesy Investors Business Daily

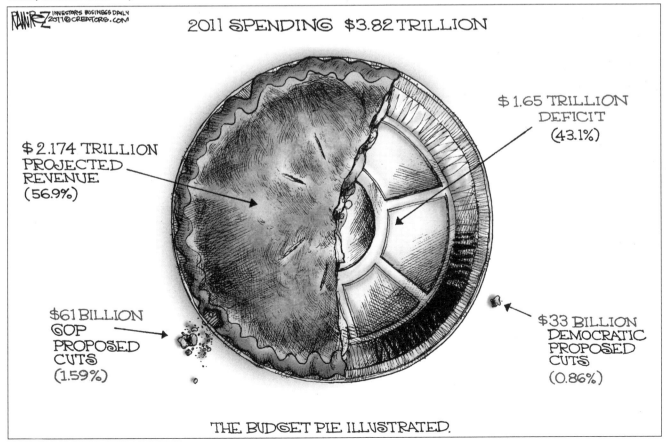

2011 SPENDING $3.82 TRILLION

$1.65 TRILLION DEFICIT (43.1%)

$2.174 TRILLION PROJECTED REVENUE (56.9%)

$61 BILLION GOP PROPOSED CUTS (1.59%)

$33 BILLION DEMOCRATIC PROPOSED CUTS (0.86%)

THE BUDGET PIE ILLUSTRATED.

BOB LANG
Courtesy Rightoons.com

TIM HARTMAN
Courtesy Beaver County Times-Record (Pa.)

J.D. CROWE
Courtesy Mobile Press-Register

MICHAEL POHRER
Courtesy National Free Press

DAN ROSANDICH
Courtesy danscartoons.com

JONATHAN RICHARDS
Courtesy Huffington Post

110

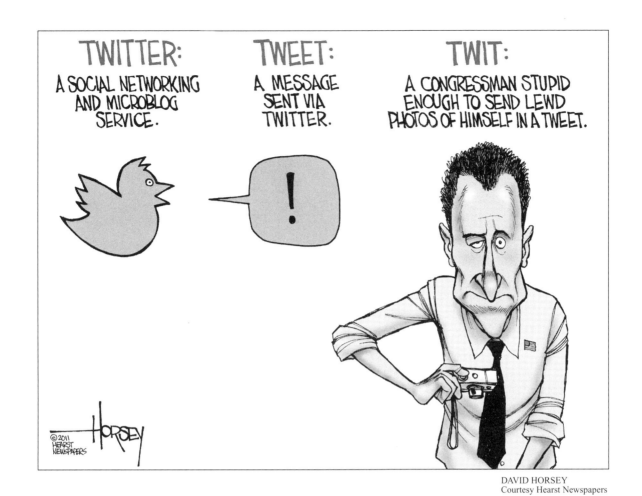

DAVID HORSEY
Courtesy Hearst Newspapers

ROBERT ENGLEHART
Courtesy Hartford Courant

Cell Phones should be held at least one inch from your body (100ft if you are a politician).

CHARLES BEYL
Courtesy Sunday News (Pa.)

JOHN SHERFFIUS
Courtesy Boulder Camera

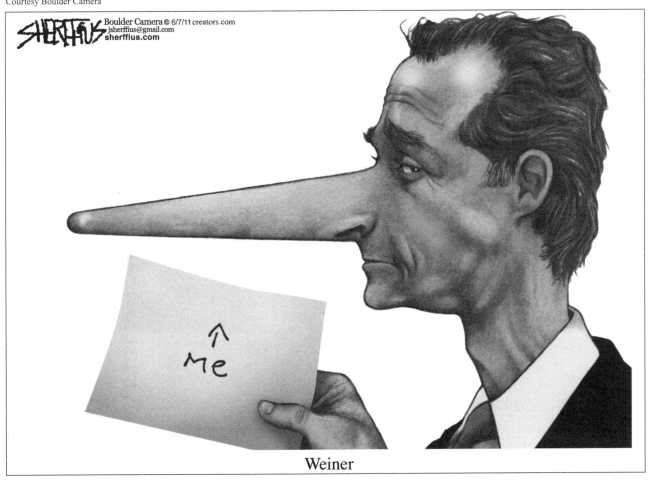

Weiner

JIMMY MARGULIES
Courtesy North Jersey Media Group

WALT HANDELSMAN
Courtesy Newsday

TIMOTHY JACKSON
Courtesy Chicago Defender

daniele@knoxnews.com

CHARLIE DANIEL
Courtesy Knoxville News-Sentinel

MIKE BECKOM
Courtesy beckomtoonz@aol.com

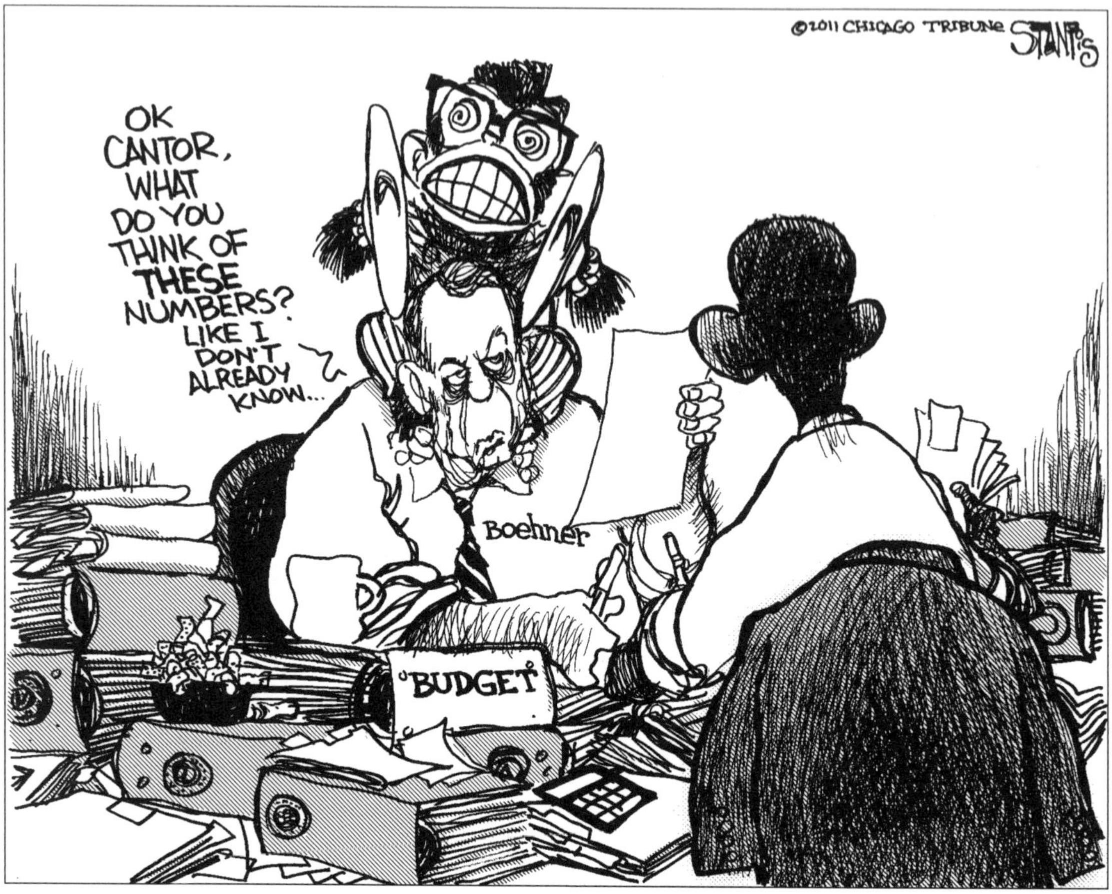
©2011 CHICAGO TRIBUNE STANTIS
OK CANTOR, WHAT DO YOU THINK OF THESE NUMBERS?
LIKE I DON'T ALREADY KNOW...
Boehner
BUDGET

SCOTT STANTIS
Courtesy Chicago Tribune

ANTHONY BAYER
Courtesy tonybayertoons.com

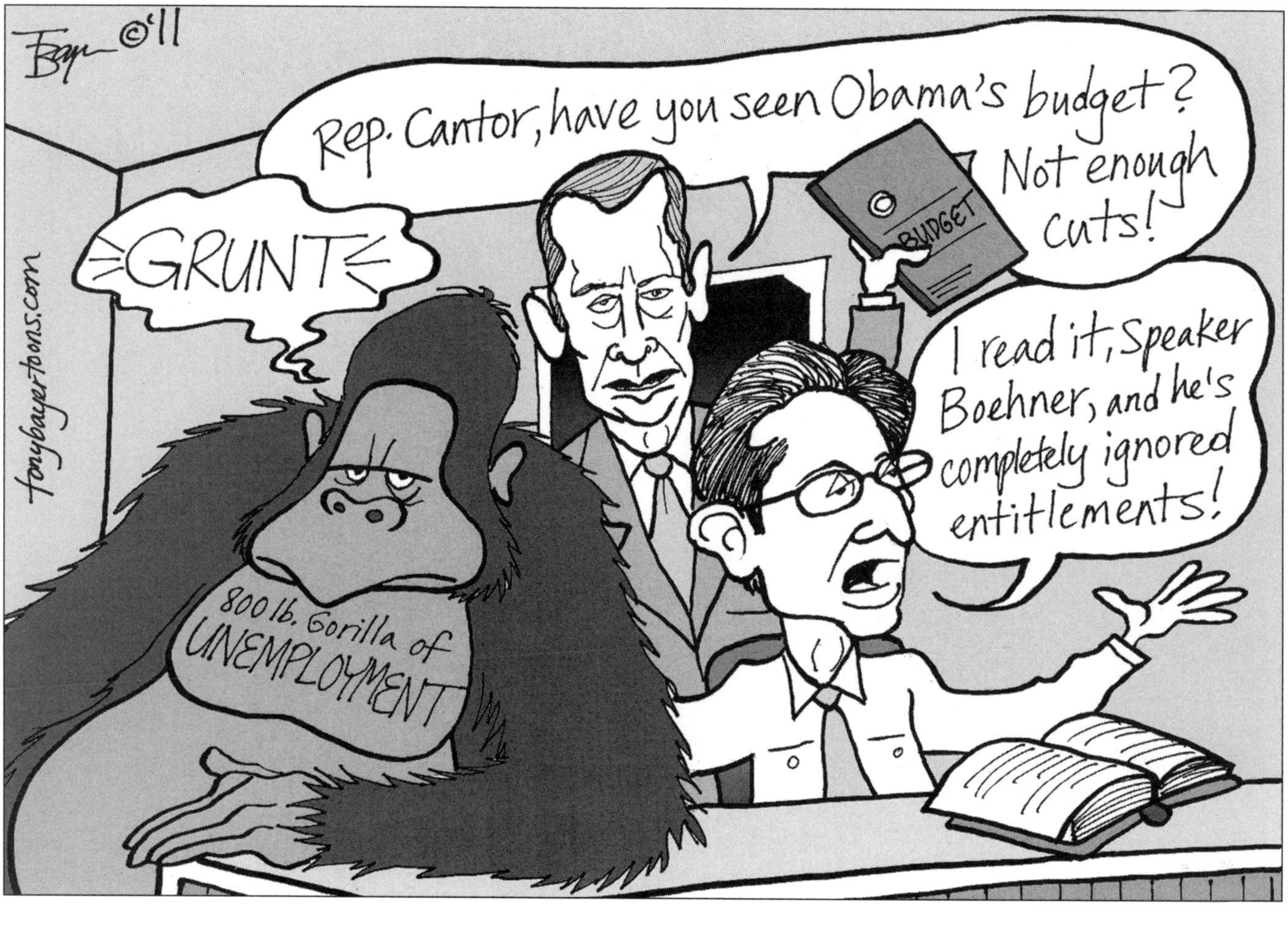
Bayer ©'11
Rep. Cantor, have you seen Obama's budget? Not enough cuts!
BUDGET
GRUNT
tonybayertoons.com
I read it, Speaker Boehner, and he's completely ignored entitlements!
800 lb. Gorilla of UNEMPLOYMENT

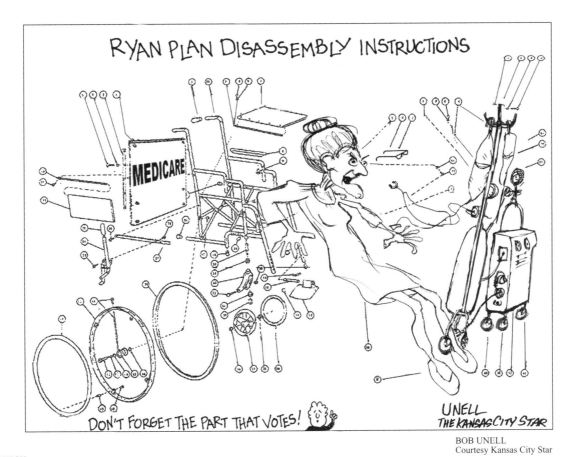

BOB UNELL
Courtesy Kansas City Star

DAVID HITCH
Courtesy Telegram & Gazette (Mass.)

JOE RANK
Courtesy Times-Press-Recorder (Calif.)

NEIL GRAHAME
Courtesy Spencer Newspapers

STEVE EDWARDS
Courtesy Gateway Journalism Review

118

WALT HANDELSMAN
Courtesy Newsday

CLAY BENNETT
Courtesy Chattanooga Times-Free Press

THE HARD RIGHT TURN

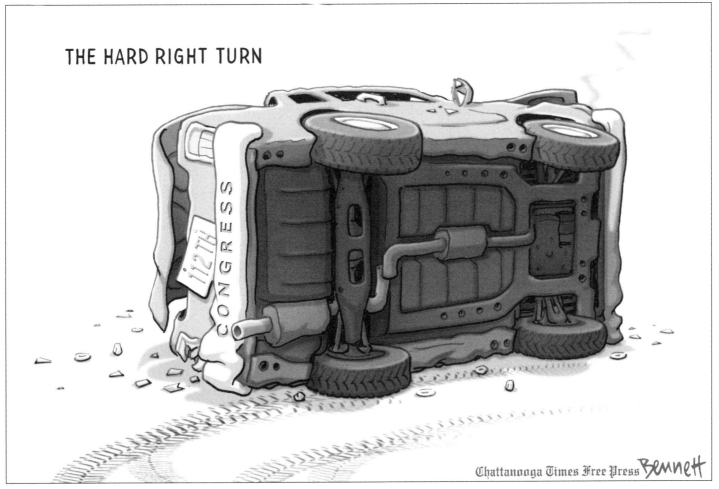

119

WILLIAM FLINT
Courtesy Dallas Morning News

MIKE BECKOM
Courtesy beckomtoonz@aol.com

Society

The U.S. remains sharply divided between red- and blue-state mentality, but many ignore politics to focus on everyday life, leisure pursuits, and social media. Digital communication now connects more and more people through texting, Facebook, Twitter, YouTube, and LinkedIn. Texting while driving has become as much a threat to highway safety as drinking.

The British royal wedding of Prince William and Catherine Middleton provided diversion from economic concerns—at least for those who could afford it. Most Americans enjoyed a peaceful Labor Day celebration, but U.S. soldiers were still fighting terrorism in Afghanistan and Iraq. Harold Camping, an 89-year-old preacher, predicted the world would end on May 21. It didn't.

Members of the Westboro Baptist Church continued their protests at the funerals of fallen soldiers. The Supreme Court ruled that Wal-Mart cannot be sued for discrimination on behalf of female workers. In a 5-4 decision, the justices ruled that lawyers pressing the case failed to prove that Wal-Mart policy led to gender discrimination.

A memorial to Dr. Martin Luther King, Jr. was erected in Washington, D.C. between the Lincoln and Jefferson memorials. Dedication was postponed because of Hurricane Irene.

MIKE LUCKOVICH
Courtesy Atlanta Journal-Constitution

TERRY C. WISE
Courtesy Ratland.com

JOEL PETT
Courtesy Lexington Herald-Leader

ED HALL
Courtesy Baker County Press (Fla.)

CHARLES BEYL
Courtesy Sunday News (Pa.)

MIKE GEMPELER
Courtesy Lee's Summit Journal

123

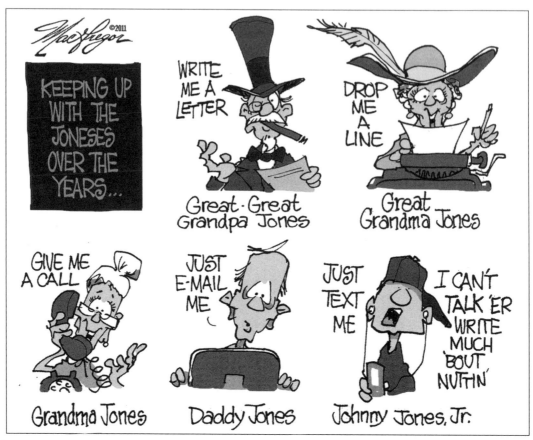

DOUG MACGREGOR
Courtesy The News-Press (Fla.)

PHIL HANDS
Courtesy Wisconsin State Journal

JIMMY MARGULIES
Courtesy North Jersey Media Group

MIKE MARLAND
Courtesy Concord Monitor

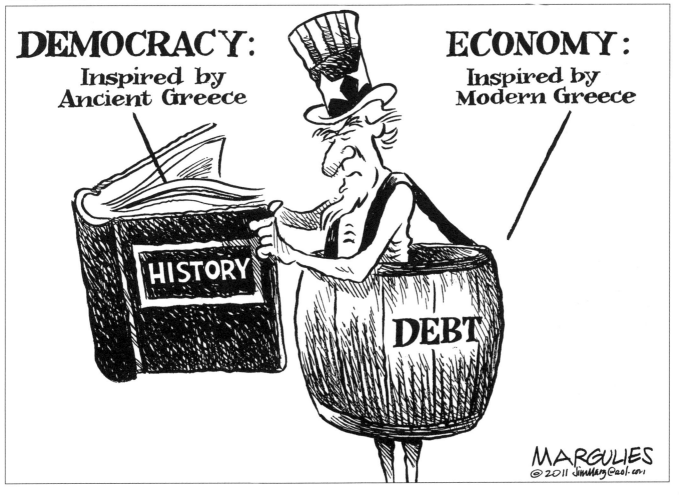

JOE RANK
Courtesy Times-Press-Recorder (Calif.)

STEVE NEASE
Courtesy Nease Cartoons

TIMOTHY JACKSON
Courtesy Chicago Defender

KEVIN SIERS
Courtesy Charlotte Observer

J.D. CROWE
Courtesy Mobile Press-Register

ROBERT ARIAIL
Courtesy Spartanburg Herald-Journal

CHAN LOWE
Courtesy Tribune Media

128

DOUG REGALIA
Courtesy MRCPA.COM

JEFF DANZIGER
Courtesy NYTS/CWS

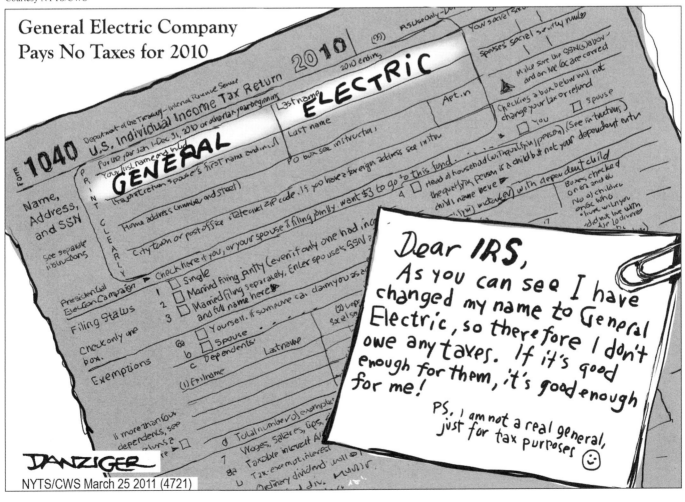

STEVE NEASE
Courtesy Nease Cartoons

GRAEME MACKAY
Courtesy Hamilton Spectator (Ont.)

FRED MULHEARN
Courtesy The Advocate (La.)

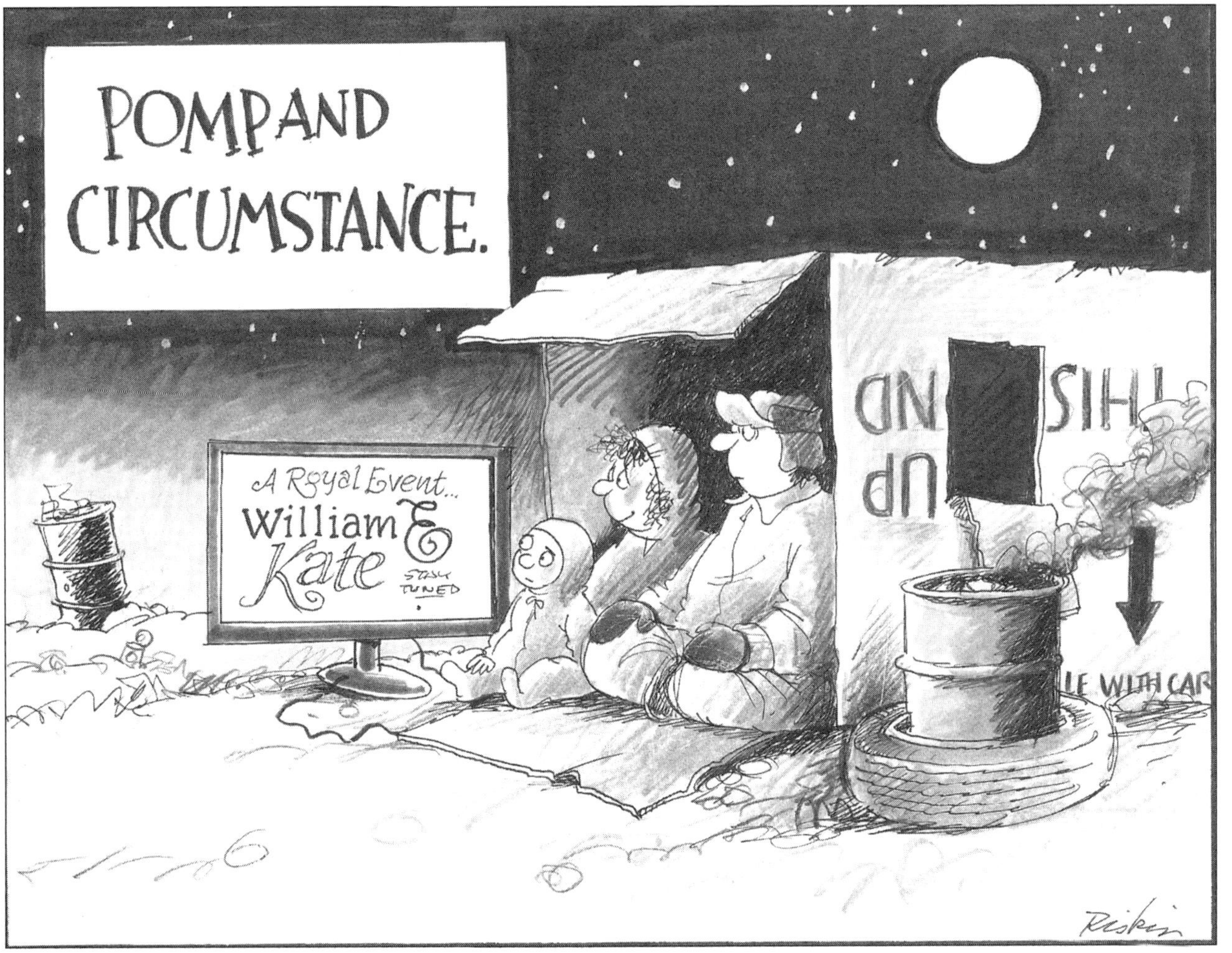
POMP AND CIRCUMSTANCE.
A Royal Event... William & Kate
STAY TUNED
Riskin

MARTY RISKIN
Courtesy Penspeakcartoons.com

STEVE EDWARDS
Courtesy Gateway Journalism Review

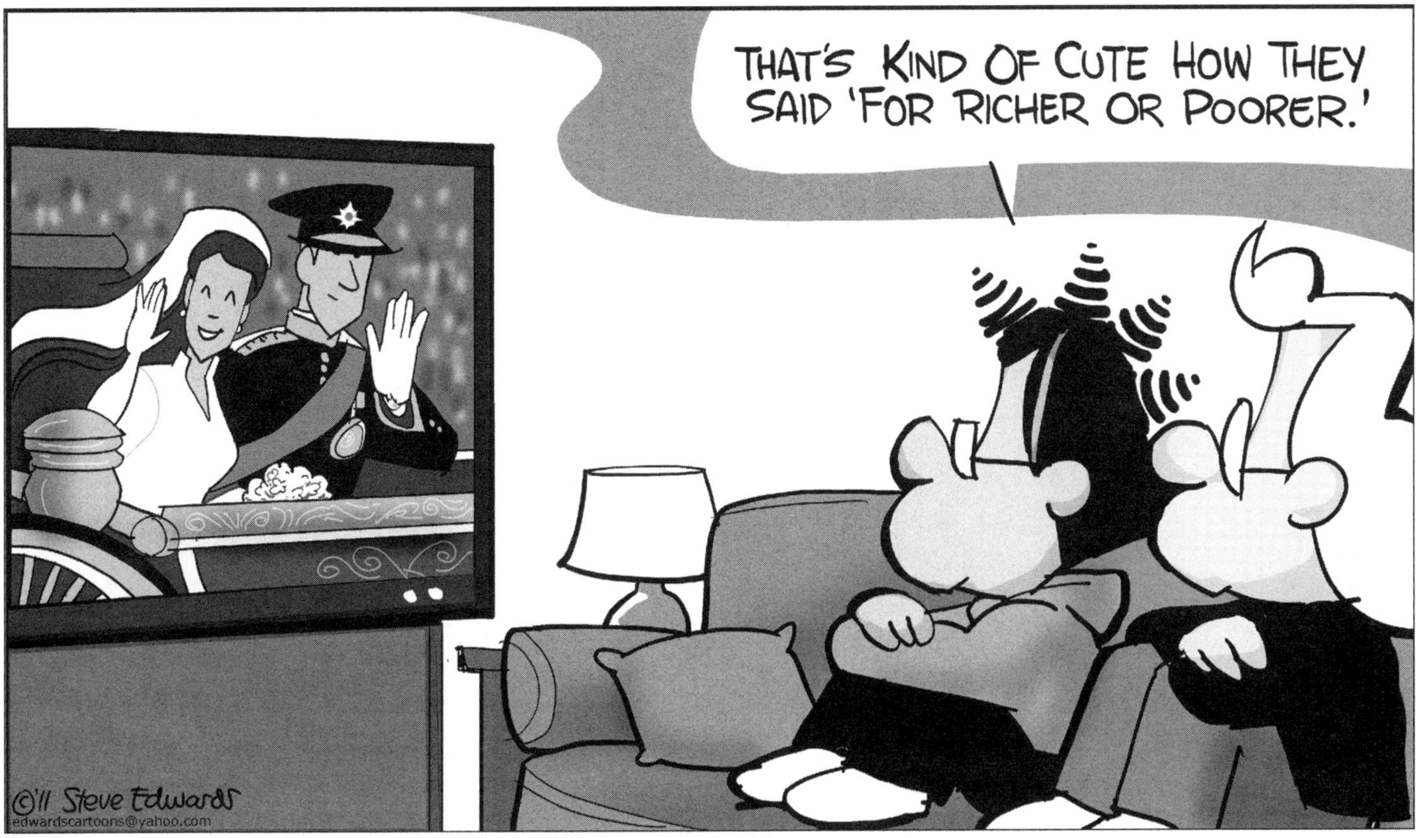
THAT'S KIND OF CUTE HOW THEY SAID 'FOR RICHER OR POORER.'
©'11 Steve Edwards
edwardscartoons@yahoo.com

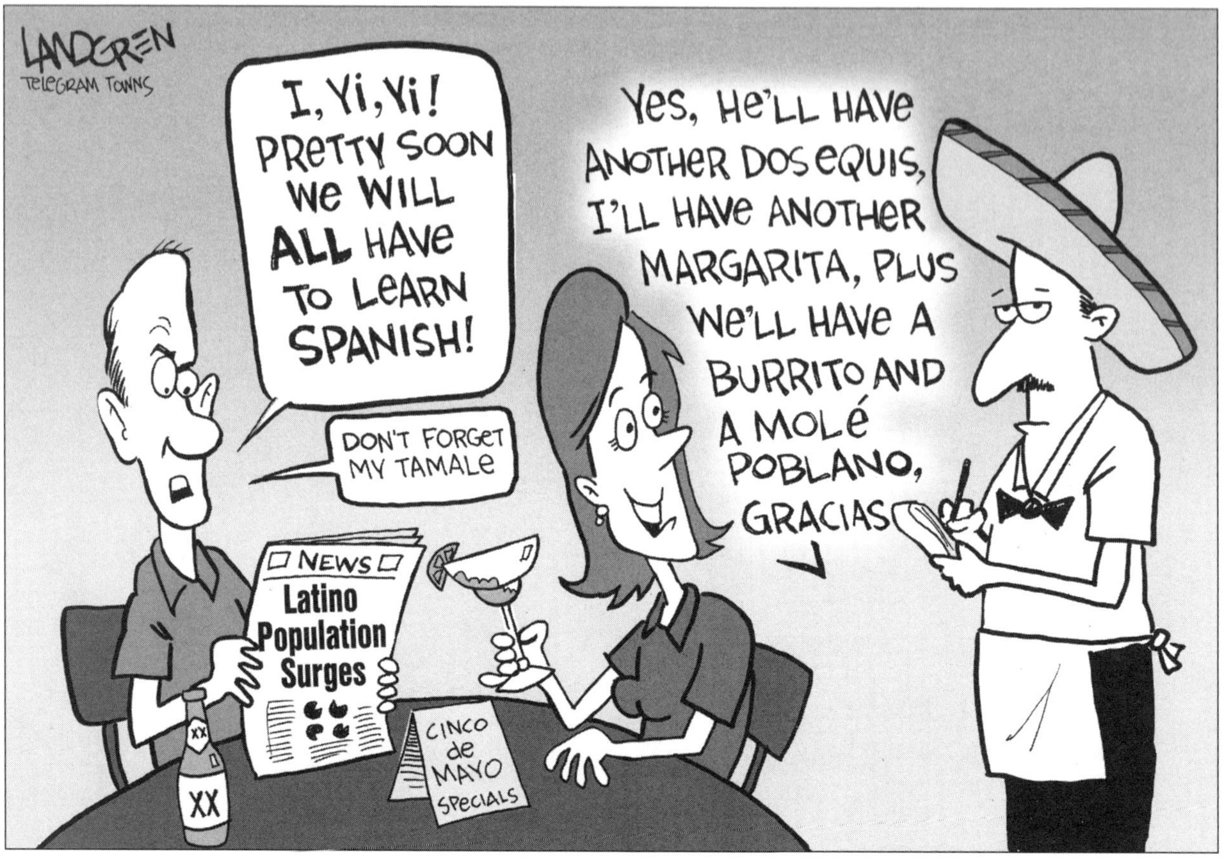
LANDGREN
TELEGRAM TOWNS
I, YI, YI! PRETTY SOON WE WILL ALL HAVE TO LEARN SPANISH!
DON'T FORGET MY TAMALE
YES, HE'LL HAVE ANOTHER DOS EQUIS, I'LL HAVE ANOTHER MARGARITA, PLUS WE'LL HAVE A BURRITO AND A MOLÉ POBLANO, GRACIAS
NEWS
Latino Population Surges
XX
CINCO de MAYO SPECIALS

DONALD E. LANDGREN JR.
Copyright Worcester Telegram & Gazette Corp.
Reprinted with permission.

GARY MARKSTEIN
Courtesy Creators Syndicate

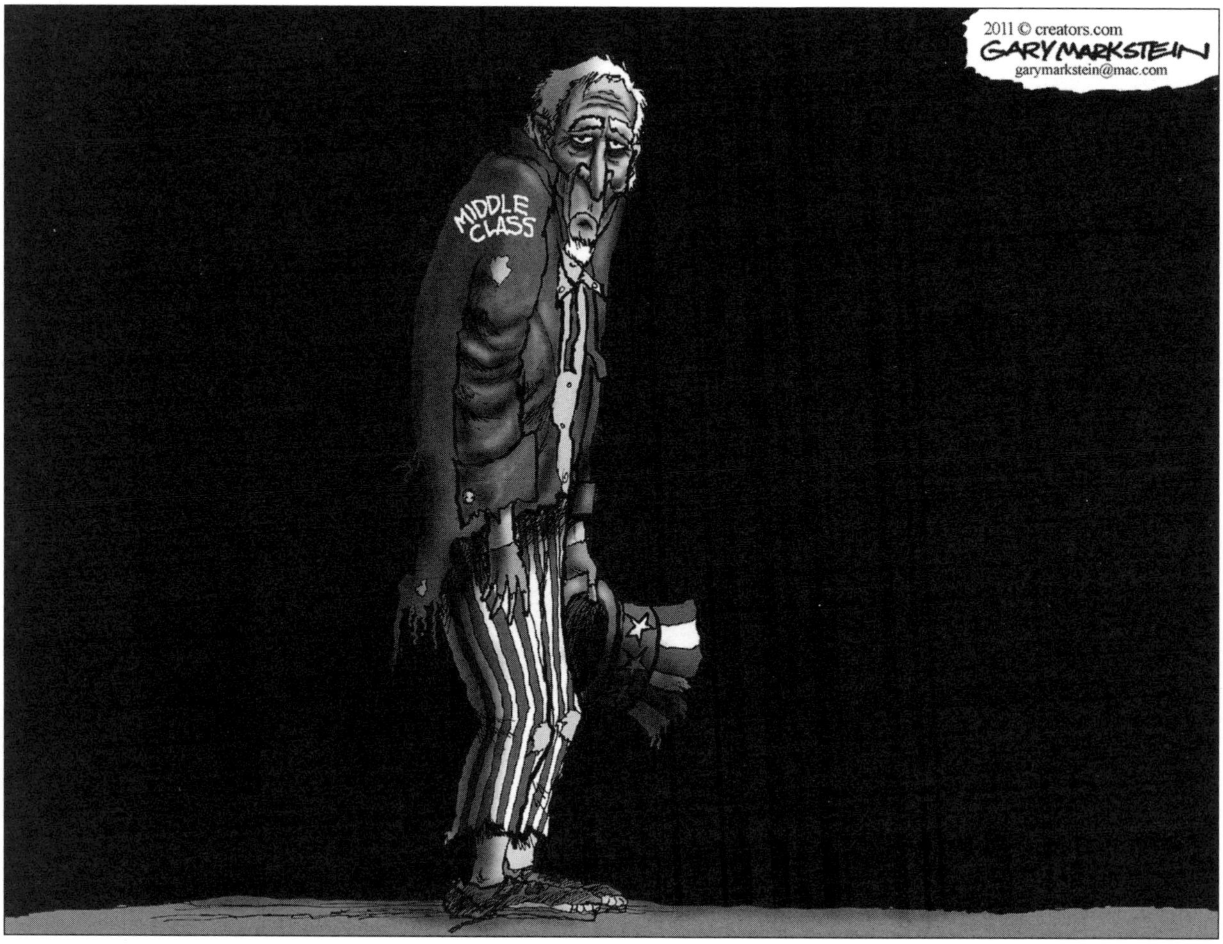
2011 © creators.com
GARY MARKSTEIN
garymarkstein@mac.com
MIDDLE CLASS

DAVE SATTLER
Courtesy Lafayette Journal and Courier (Ind.)

STEVEN G. ARTLEY
Courtesy artleytoons.com

STEVEN PARRA
Courtesy Fresno Bee

JOE HELLER
Courtesy Green Bay Press-Gazette

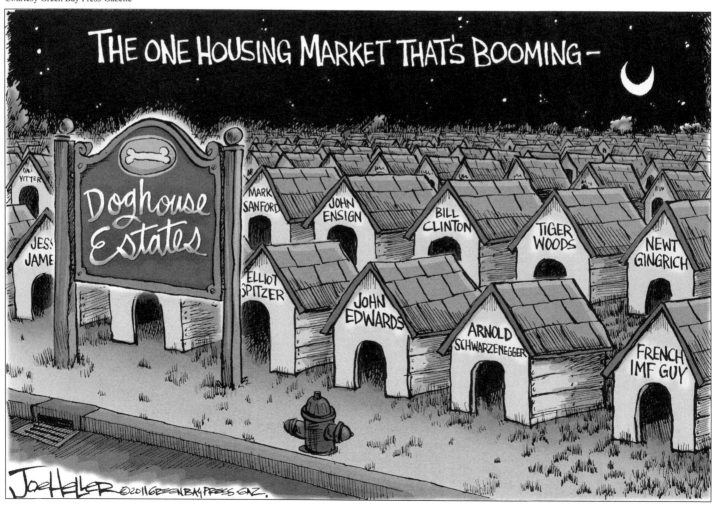

134

Media/Entertainment

The TV-watching public was fascinated by the spectacle of actor Charlie Sheen's self-destructive behavior. Sheen, infamous for alleged orgies and drug and alcohol abuse, was fired from the popular TV show "Two and a Half Men." Sheen sued Warner Brothers and appeared on YouTube, proclaiming his "victory." Actor Ashton Kutcher was eventually chosen to fill Sheen's spot on the show.

Media mogul Rupert Murdoch gave testimony before a British parliamentary committee regarding phone hacking allegedly carried out by representatives of a company he owns.

The proliferation of electronic media has cut into book sales, forcing many bookstores out of business. Former Vice President Dick Cheney wrote a book about the internal policy battles in the Bush White House. Some of his observations upset former Bush staffers.

House Republicans proposed several spending cuts to help balance the federal budget, including cutting federal funding for the Corporation for Public Broadcasting. Conservative talk show host Glenn Beck's TV program, which often criticized President Obama, was canceled by Fox.

English singer-songwriter Amy Winehouse, whose extreme lifestyle included drugs, alcohol, and outrageous antics, passed away. Steve Jobs, co-founder of Apple, announced his resignation as company CEO and died in October.

CHUCK ASAY
Courtesy Creators.com

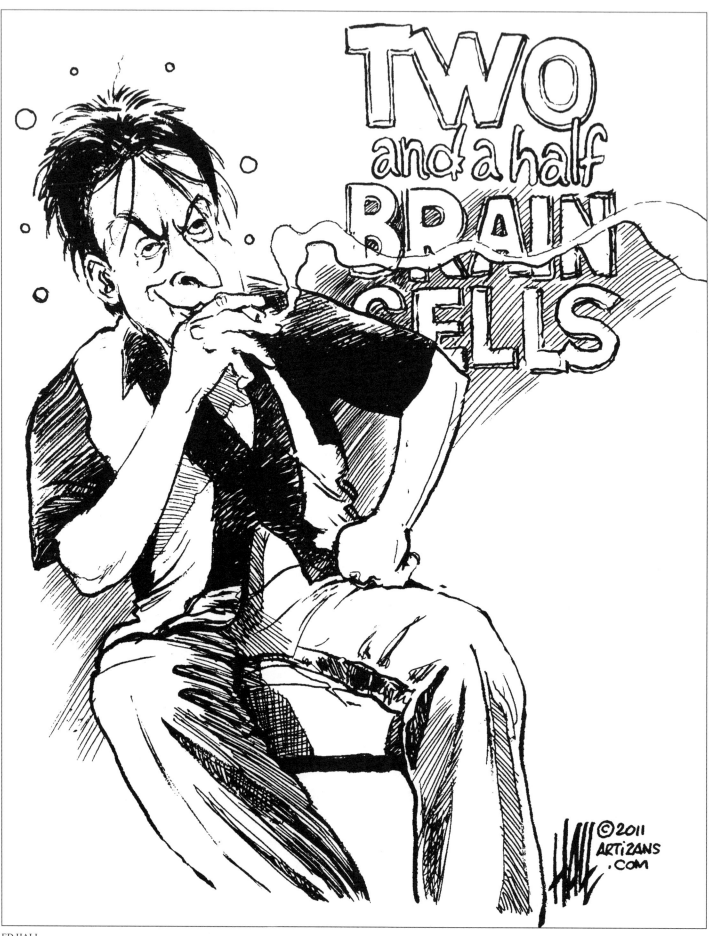

TWO and a half BRAIN CELLS

©2011
ARTiZANS
.COM

136

MIKE KEEFE
Courtesy Denver Post

DAVID HITCH
Courtesy Telegram & Gazette (Mass.)

137

CORE OF THE APPLE

STEVE BREEN
Courtesy San Diego Union-Tribune

BRUCE PLANTE
Courtesy Tulsa World

iSad

"I could re-design that for you."

JIM BERTRAM
Courtesy St. Cloud Times (Minn.)

JOHN ROSE
Courtesy Byrd Newspapers of Virginia

139

JOHN AUCHTER
Courtesy Grand Rapids Press

HAP PITKIN
Courtesy Boulder Camera

Cheney explains.

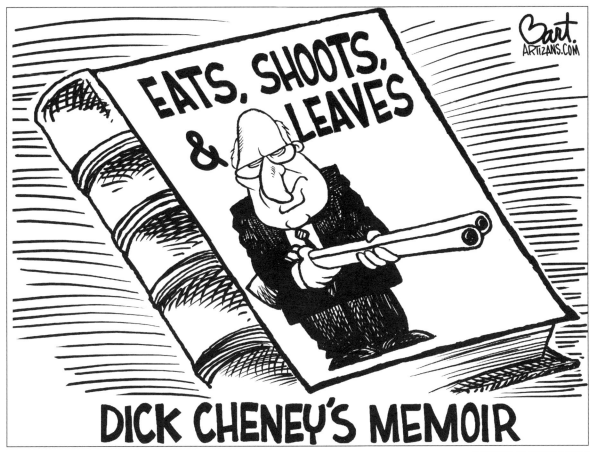

RICHARD BARTHOLOMEW
Courtesy Artizans Syndicate

MIKE LUCKOVICH
Courtesy Atlanta Journal-Constitution

CHUCK LEGGE
Courtesy Artizans.com

PAUL BERGE
Courtesy Q Syndicate

WILLIAM WARREN
Courtesy Liberty Features Syndicate

STEVE EDWARDS
Courtesy Gateway Journalism Review

ED HALL
Courtesy Baker County Press (Fla.)

TIM DOLIGHAN
Courtesy Dolighan Cartoons

STEVE EDWARDS
Courtesy Gateway Journalism Review

144

JAY SCHILLER and GREG CRAVENS
Courtesy McClatchy-Tribune Campus

STEVE KELLEY
Courtesy The Times-Picayune (La.)

KEN VEGOTSKY
Courtesy Bucks County Courier-Times (Pa.)

JOHN ROSE
Courtesy Byrd Newspapers of Virginia

146

JOHN SHERFFIUS
Courtesy Boulder Camera

STEVEN PARRA
Courtesy Fresno Bee

STEVEN G. ARTLEY
Courtesy artleytoons.com

JIM DYKE
Courtesy Jefferson City News-Tribune

Sports

Disagreements between owners and players threatened to cancel the 2011 NFL football season. After four and a half months, the NFL lockout came to an end when players and owners approved a final labor settlement, paving the way for a new 10-year collective bargaining agreement. The legal fight began when a group of players headlined by New England Patriots quarterback Tom Brady filed an antitrust lawsuit against the league. The lockout began the next day.

College football is a multimillion dollar industry. Many feel that college athletes should be paid. After a yearlong investigation, the NCAA filed a series of charges against the University of North Carolina, alleging among other things that student athletes were given impermissible benefits.

Super Bowl XLV between the Pittsburgh Steelers and Green Bay Packers was a pricey event. One fan reportedly spent $70,000 for a suite inside Cowboys Stadium. The average ticket price was reported to be between $2,100 and $8,000. The Packers were triumphant, 31-25.

The Houston Astros suffered the worst season in the history of the baseball franchise. They lost to the St. Louis Cardinals 8-0 in the final game of the season. The Cardinals won the World Series in seven games over the Texas Rangers.

WILLIAM FLINT
Courtesy Dallas Morning News

DENNIS DRAUGHON
Courtesy Fayetteville Observer

WILL O'TOOLE
Courtesy Otoons

JOE GROSHEK
Courtesy Joe Groshek

WILL O'TOOLE
Courtesy Otoons

DAVE SATTLER
Courtesy Lafayette Journal and Courier (Ind.)

THOMAS BECK
Courtesy Freeport Journal-Standard (Ill.)

KARL WIMER
Courtesy Denver Business Journal

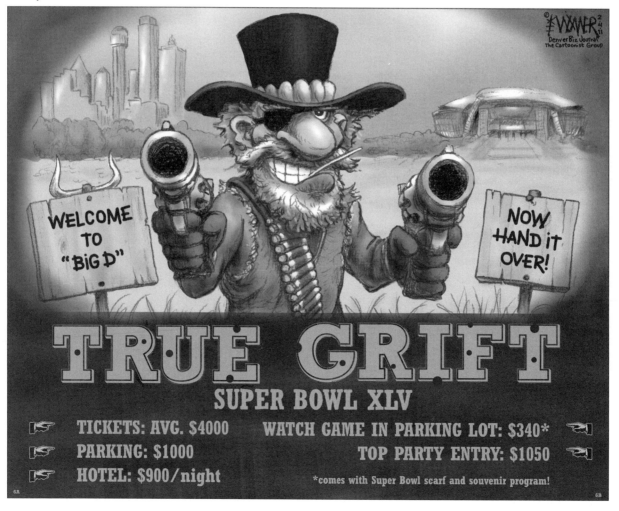

Health/Education

Legal challenges began chipping away at the Obama health care reform law. The plaintiffs in a 26-state challenge to the law asked the Supreme Court to take up the case during its upcoming term. Opponents say the law is unconstitutional because it requires citizens to purchase health insurance. Two appeals courts have issued opposing rulings on the law's individual mandate, increasing the likelihood that the high court will decide to weigh in.

U.S. students continue to lag behind much of the rest of the world in mathematics and science, adding to the problem of unemployment. Many businessmen complained that they had jobs to fill but couldn't find qualified employees. In some states, budget cuts put further pressure on education. America's education advantage, unrivaled in the years after World War II, is eroding quickly, according to some experts.

Students in other countries are graduating from high school and college with higher achievement scores than students in the U.S. Some pundits have even suggested that the benefits of higher education have been oversold. They argue that a good high school education is sufficient for most.

Dysfunctional families and a culture that undervalues education were also seen as problems for U.S. students, who have been called "over-entertained" and "distracted" by electronic gadgets.

GARY VARVEL
Courtesy Indianapolis Star

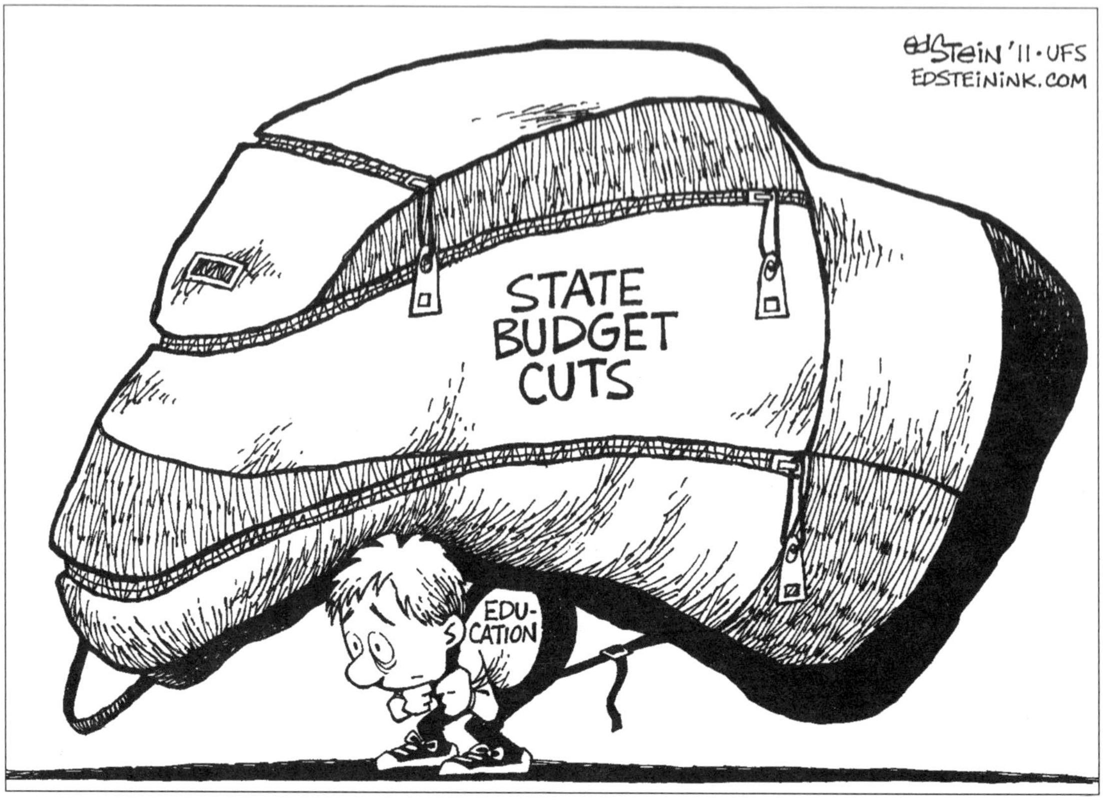
EdStein '11 · UFS
EDSTEININK.COM
STATE BUDGET CUTS
EDU-CATION

ED STEIN
Courtesy EDSTEININK.COM

PAUL FELL
Courtesy Artizans Syndicate

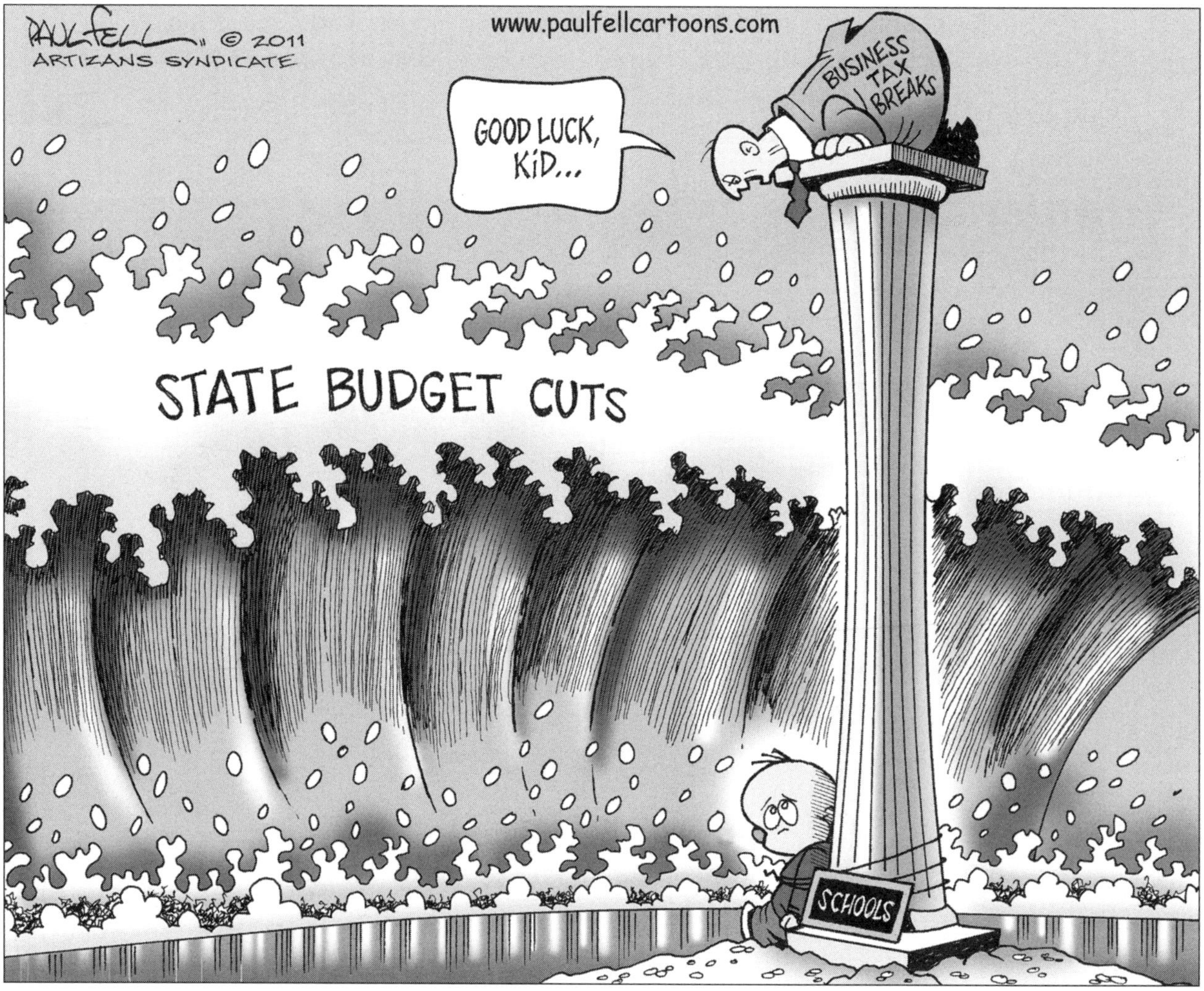
PAUL FELL © 2011
ARTIZANS SYNDICATE
www.paulfellcartoons.com
BUSINESS TAX BREAKS
GOOD LUCK, KID...
STATE BUDGET CUTS
SCHOOLS

TOM TOLES

STEVE GREENBERG
Courtesy Ventura County Reporter (Calif.)

MIKE GEMPELER
Courtesy Lee's Summit Journal

DAVE SATTLER
Courtesy Lafayette Journal and Courier (Ind.)

ANNETTE BALESTERI
Courtesy The News (Calif.)

WILLIAM FLINT
Courtesy Dallas Morning News

ED GAMBLE
Courtesy King Features Syndicate

STEVEN PARRA
Courtesy Fresno Bee

JESSE SPRINGER
Courtesy Eugene Register-Guard

S.O.S.! (SAVE OUR SCHOOLS!)

JERRY GARDEN
Courtesy GardenARToons(Calif.)

MICHAEL POHRER
Courtesy National Free Press

STEVE NEASE
Courtesy Nease Cartoons

JOHN AUCHTER
Courtesy Grand Rapids Press

160

JIM MCCLOSKEY
Courtesy The News-Leader (Va.)

PHIL HANDS
Courtesy Wisconsin State Journal

JOHN BRANCH
Courtesy Branchtoon.com/
    North American Syndicate

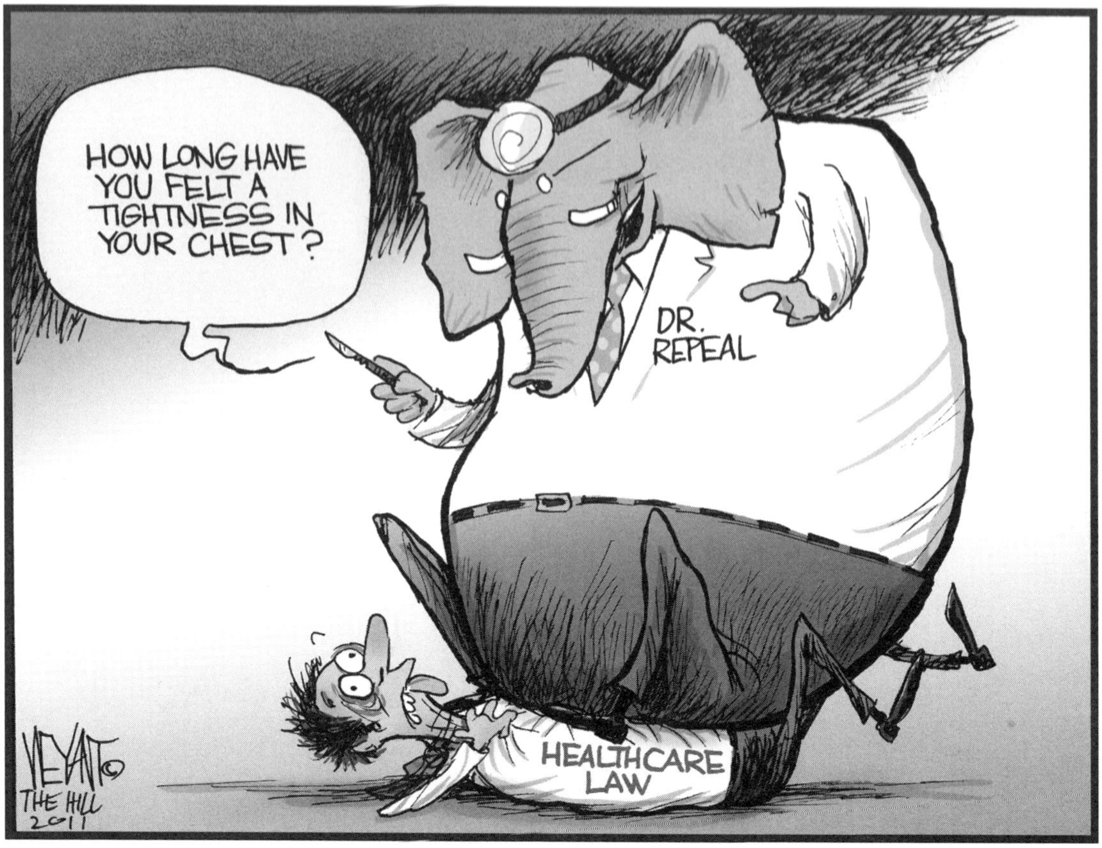
HOW LONG HAVE YOU FELT A TIGHTNESS IN YOUR CHEST?
DR. REPEAL
HEALTHCARE LAW
WEYANT© THE HILL 2011

CHRIS WEYANT
Courtesy The Hill

LISA BENSON
Courtesy Washington Post Writers Group

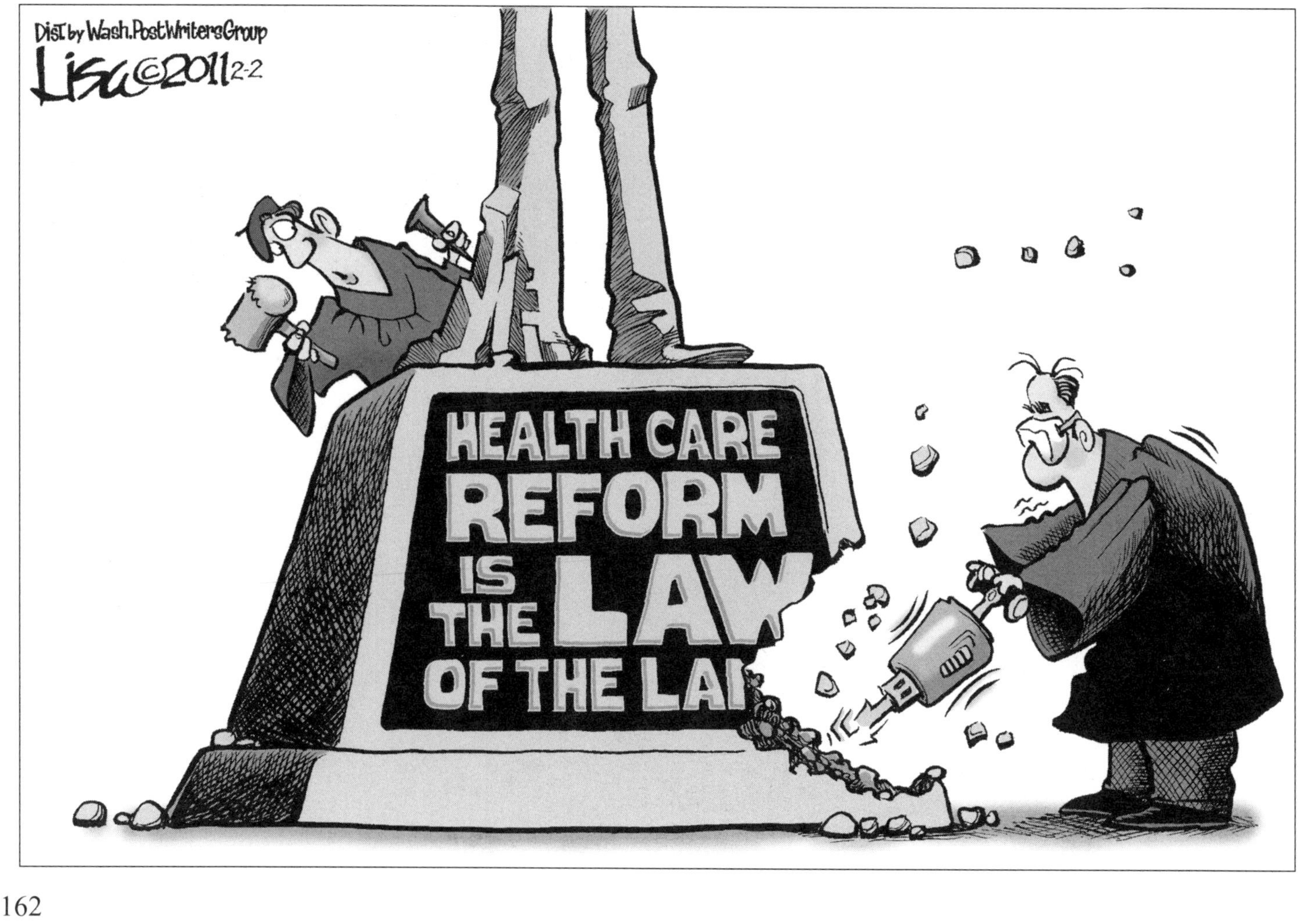
Dist by Wash. Post Writers Group
Lisa ©2011 2-2
HEALTH CARE REFORM IS THE LAW OF THE LA

The Environment

President Obama made green jobs a centerpiece of his administration, but the failure of Solyndra, a solar panel manufacturer, jeopardized the program. The company received more than half a billion dollars in federal loan guarantees before going bankrupt. Obama angered environmentalists by easing air pollution regulations and approving a pipeline from Canada to the Texas Gulf Coast.

A rare East Coast hurricane, Irene, caused flooding and destruction from North Carolina to Vermont. Millions were left without power, and many flights were canceled. A massive thunderstorm front spawned 137 tornadoes in the South, killing 180. Another tornado devastated Joplin, Missouri. Two major storms dumped record rainfall, swelling the Mississippi River.

A drought in some of California's most fertile farmland ended when winter storms piled snow up to three stories high. Thousands of birds died and dropped from the skies over Arkansas and Louisiana, baffling wildlife experts. The Gulf Coast continued to recover from the effects of the BP oil spill. Confidence in nuclear power was shaken by an earthquake and tsunami in Japan and by another earthquake in Virginia. Both incidents resulted in the shutdown of nuclear power plants.

Canadian filmmaker James Cameron, whose film credits include *Terminator* and *Titanic,* toured the Alberta oil sands with premier Edward Stelmach.

ANOTHER FEEL GOOD MOMENT

CHIP BOK
Courtesy Creators Syndicate

ROBERT ENGLEHART
Courtesy Hartford Courant

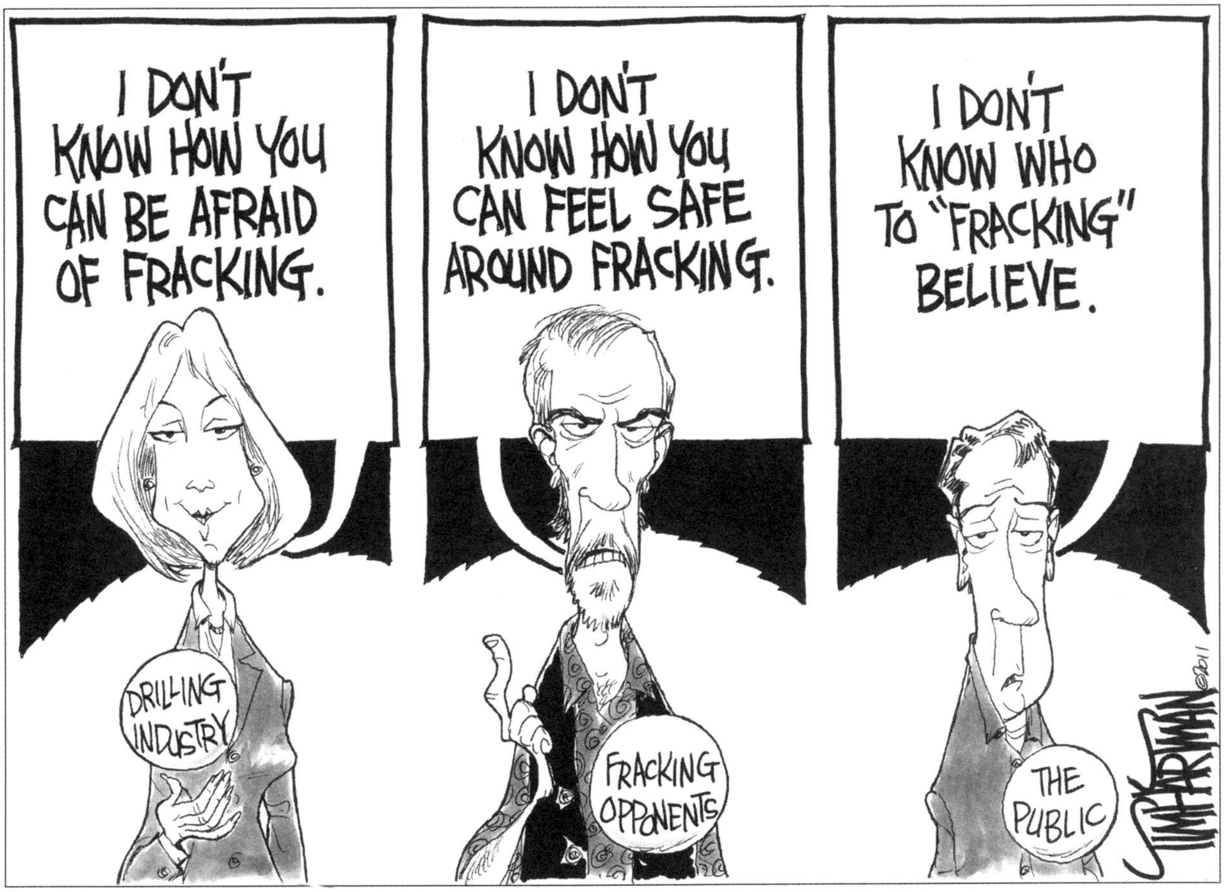
I DON'T KNOW HOW YOU CAN BE AFRAID OF FRACKING.
DRILLING INDUSTRY
I DON'T KNOW HOW YOU CAN FEEL SAFE AROUND FRACKING.
FRACKING OPPONENTS
I DON'T KNOW WHO TO "FRACKING" BELIEVE.
THE PUBLIC
TIM HARTMAN ©2011

TIM HARTMAN
Courtesy Beaver County Times-Record (Pa.)

STEVE GREENBERG
Courtesy Ventura County Reporter (Calif.)

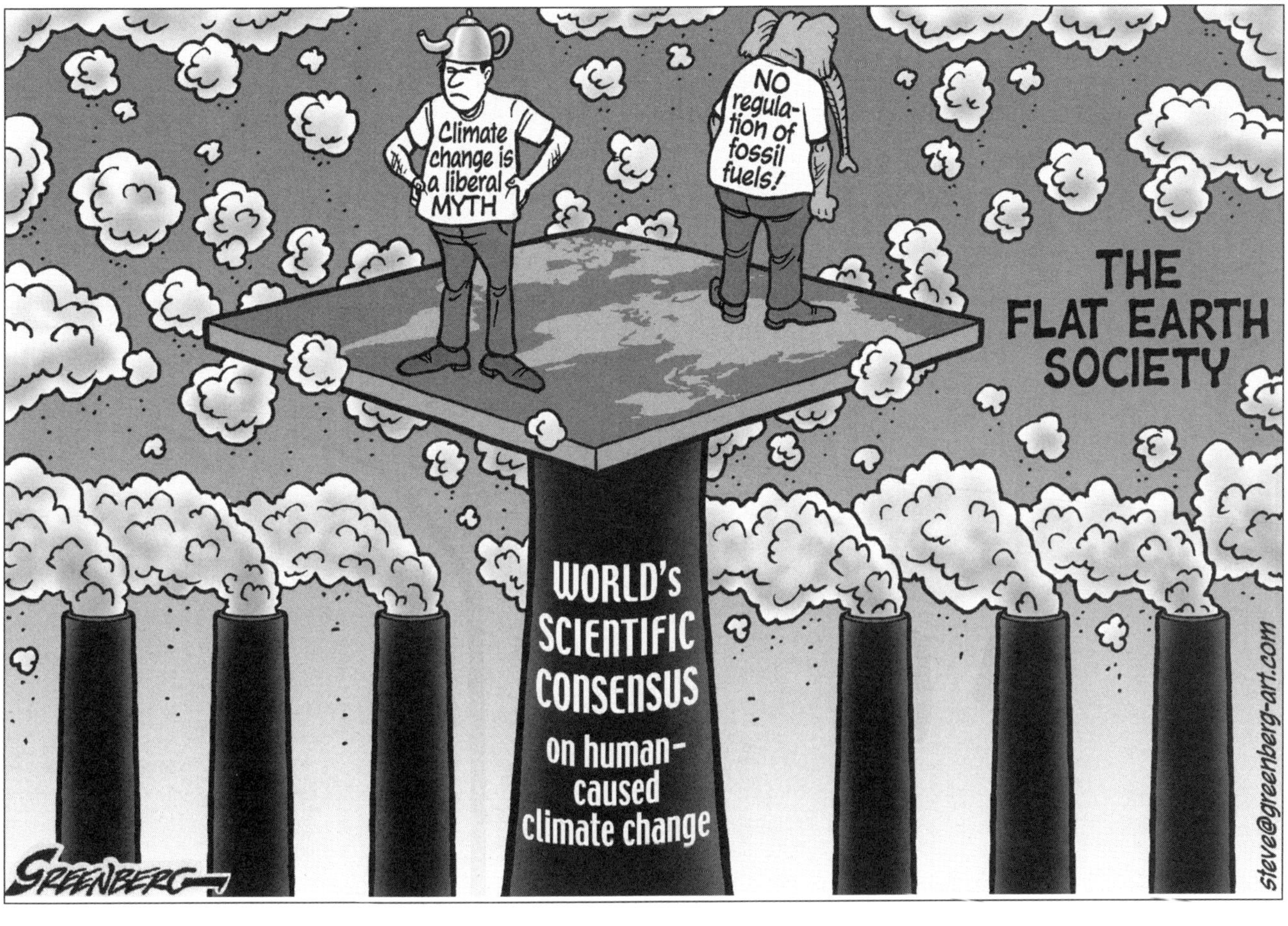
Climate change is a liberal MYTH
NO regulation of fossil fuels!
THE FLAT EARTH SOCIETY
WORLD's SCIENTIFIC CONSENSUS on human-caused climate change
GREENBERG
steve@greenberg-art.com

STEPHANIE MCMILLAN
Courtesy Code Green

DICK WALLMEYER
Courtesy Long Beach Press-Telegram

DENNIS DRAUGHON
Courtesy Fayetteville Observer

STEVE MCBRIDE
Courtesy The Reporter

RICK MCKEE
Courtesy Augusta Chronicle

CHRIS BRITT
Courtesy State Journal-Register (Ill.)

JOHN SHERFFIUS
Courtesy Boulder Camera

The killer returns

ELIZABETH BRICQUET
Courtesy Kingsport Times-News

ADAM ZYGLIS
Courtesy Buffalo News

IRENE OLDS
Courtesy The Democrat (Ind.)

JOHN ROSE
Courtesy Byrd Newspapers of Virginia

NEIL GRAHAME
Courtesy Spencer Newspapers

STEPHANIE MCMILLAN
Courtesy Code Green

JOE HELLER
Courtesy Green Bay Press-Gazette

PETER EVANS
Courtesy The Islander News (Fla.)

MARC MURPHY
Courtesy Louisville Courier-Journal

JIM DYKE
Courtesy Jefferson City News-Tribune

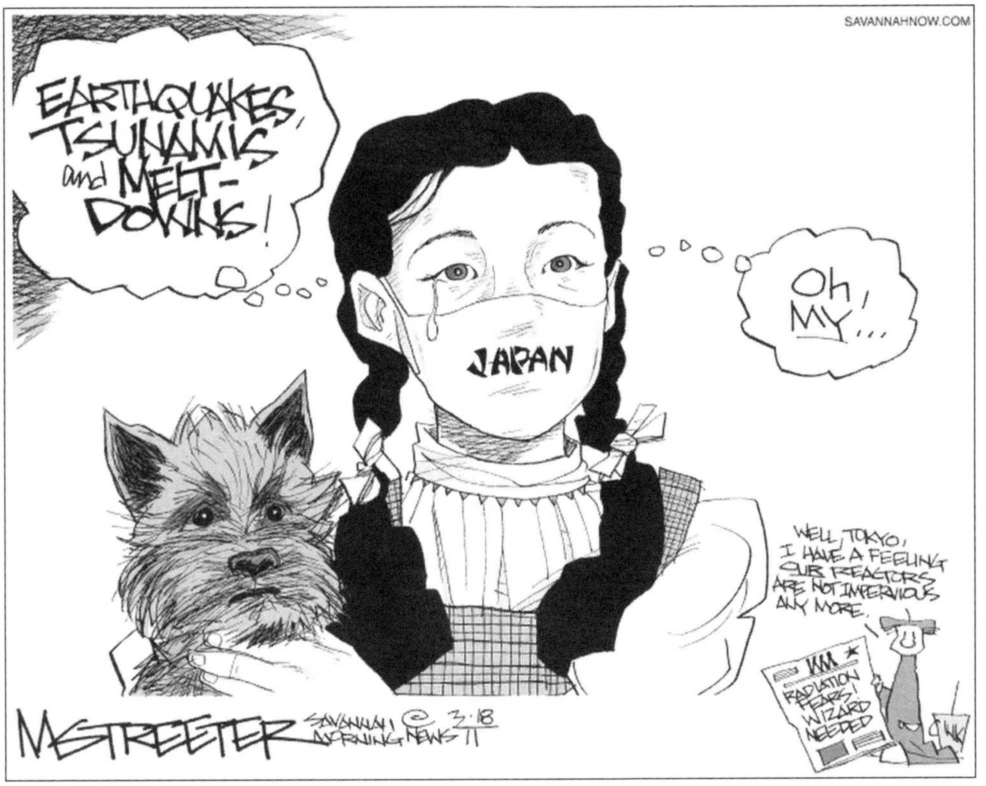
SAVANNAHNOW.COM
EARTHQUAKES, TSUNAMIS and MELT-DOWNS!
JAPAN
Oh, MY!...
WELL, TOKYO, I HAVE A FEELING OUR REACTORS ARE NOT IMPERVIOUS ANY MORE.
RADIATION FEARS! WIZARD NEEDED
MSTREETER SAVANNAH MORNING NEWS © 3·18 '11

MARK STREETER
Courtesy Savannah Morning News

ROB ROGERS
Courtesy Pittsburgh Post-Gazette

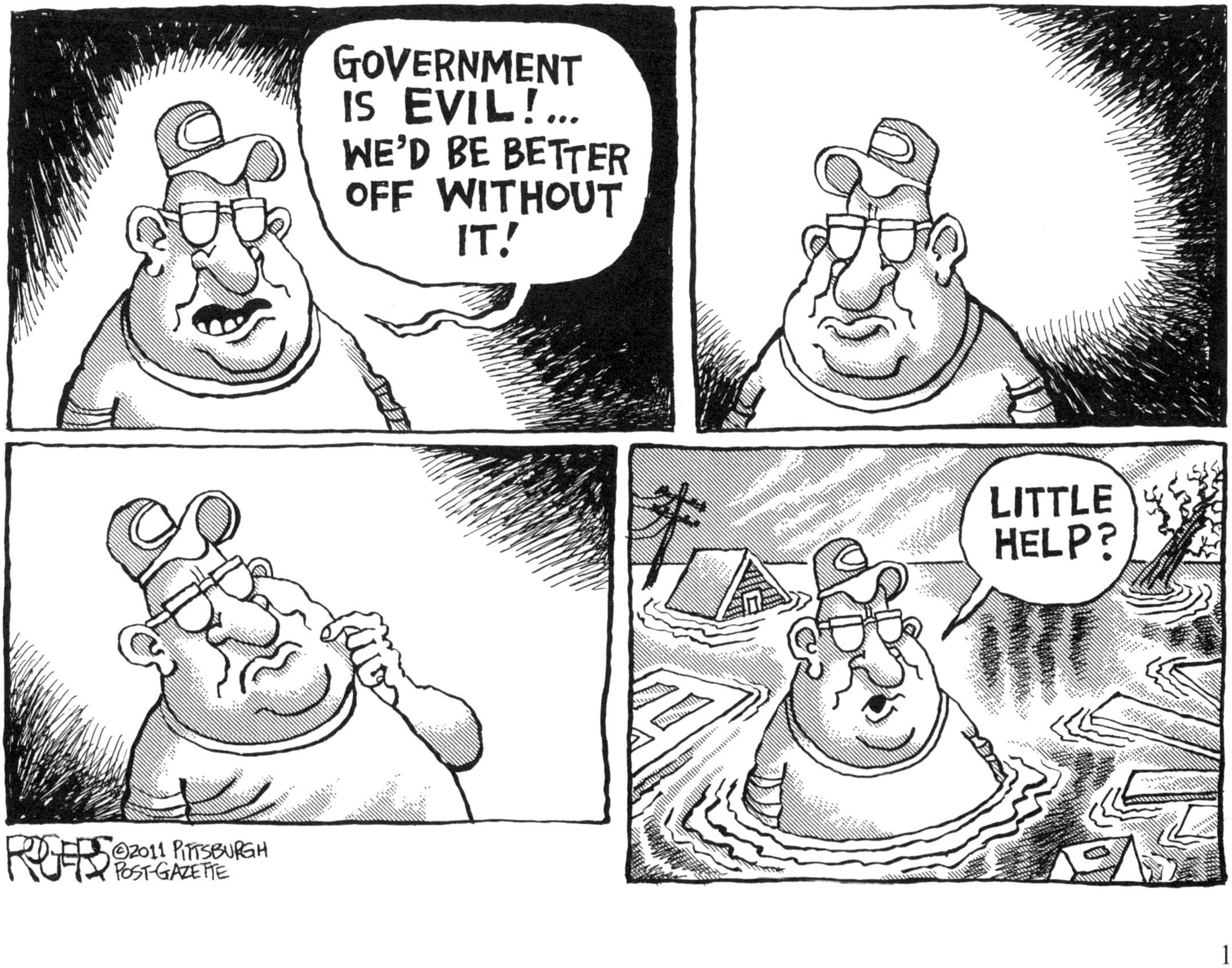
GOVERNMENT IS EVIL!... WE'D BE BETTER OFF WITHOUT IT!
LITTLE HELP?
ROGERS ©2011 PITTSBURGH POST-GAZETTE

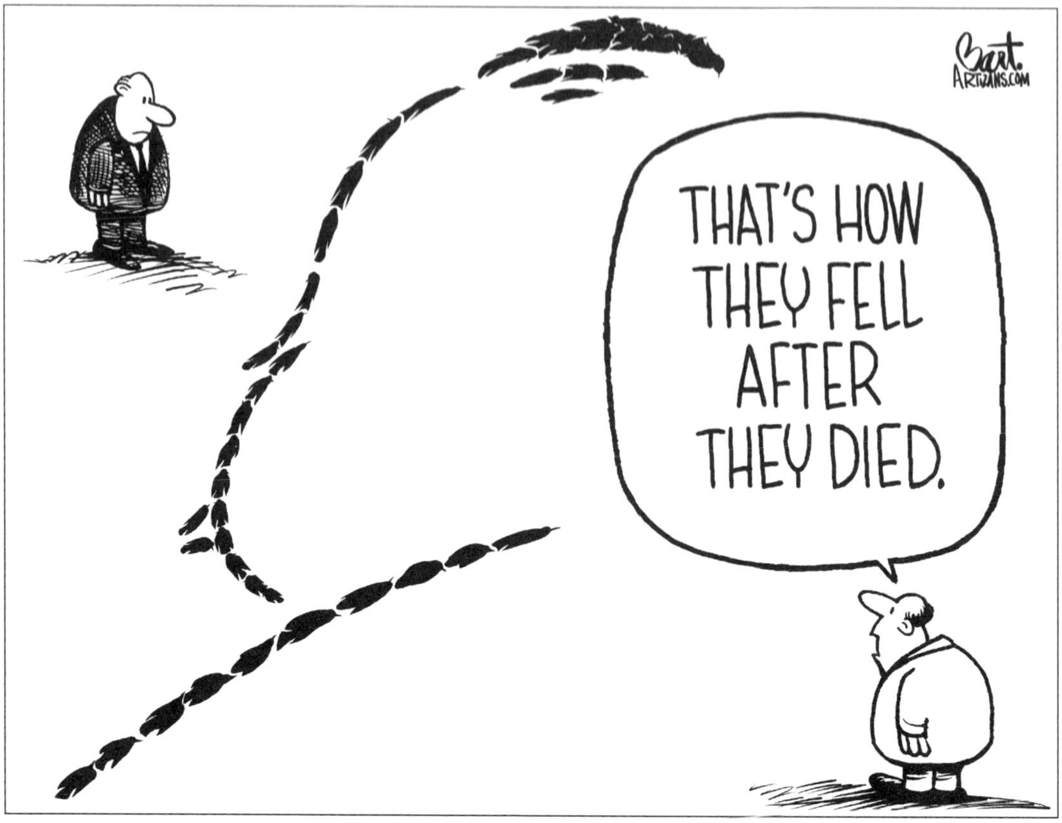
Bart.
ARTIZANS.COM
THAT'S HOW THEY FELL AFTER THEY DIED.

DONALD E. LANDGREN JR.
Copyright Worcester Telegram & Gazette Corp.
Reprinted with permission.

RICHARD BARTHOLOMEW
Courtesy Artizans Syndicate

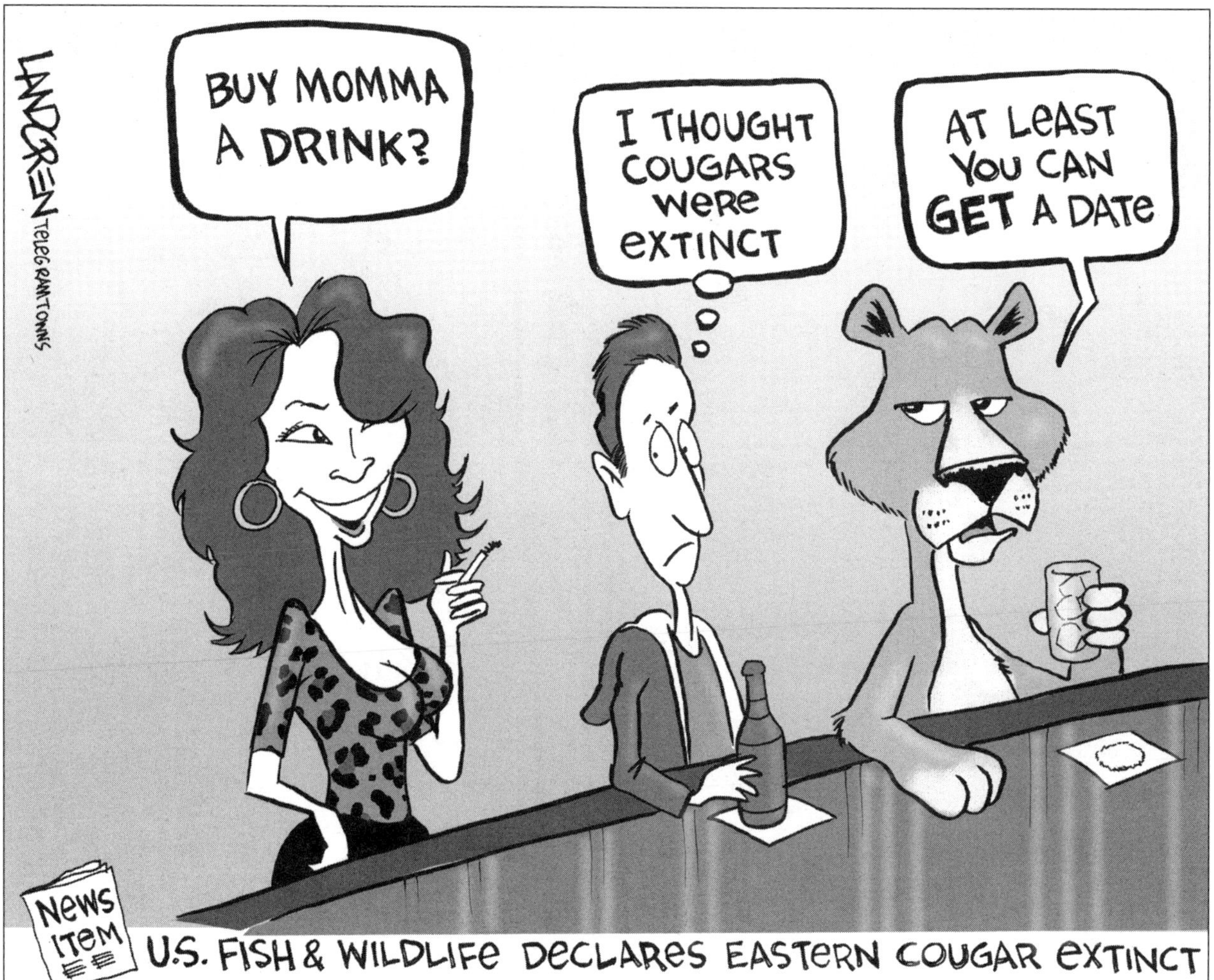
LANDGREN
TELEGRAMTOONS
BUY MOMMA A DRINK?
I THOUGHT COUGARS were EXTINCT
AT LEAST YOU CAN GET A DATE
NEWS ITEM
U.S. FISH & WILDLIFE DECLARES EASTERN COUGAR EXTINCT

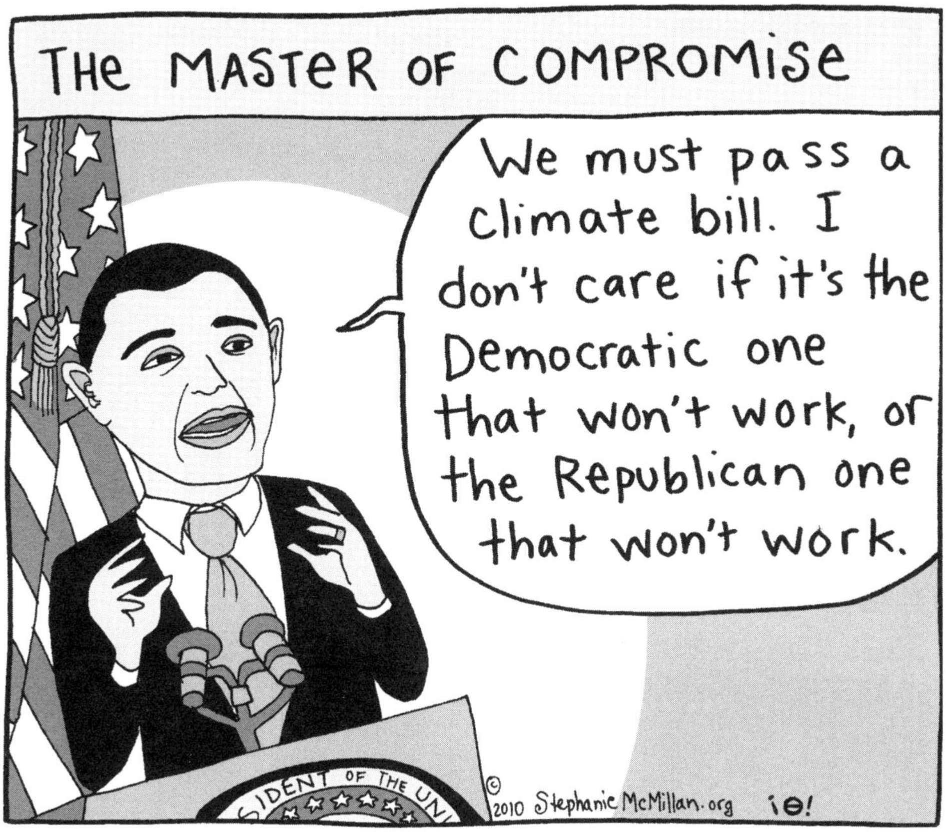
THE MASTER OF COMPROMISE
We must pass a climate bill. I don't care if it's the Democratic one that won't work, or the Republican one that won't work.
© 2010 StephanieMcMillan.org

STEPHANIE MCMILLAN
Courtesy Code Green

FRED CURATOLO
Courtesy SEE Magazine

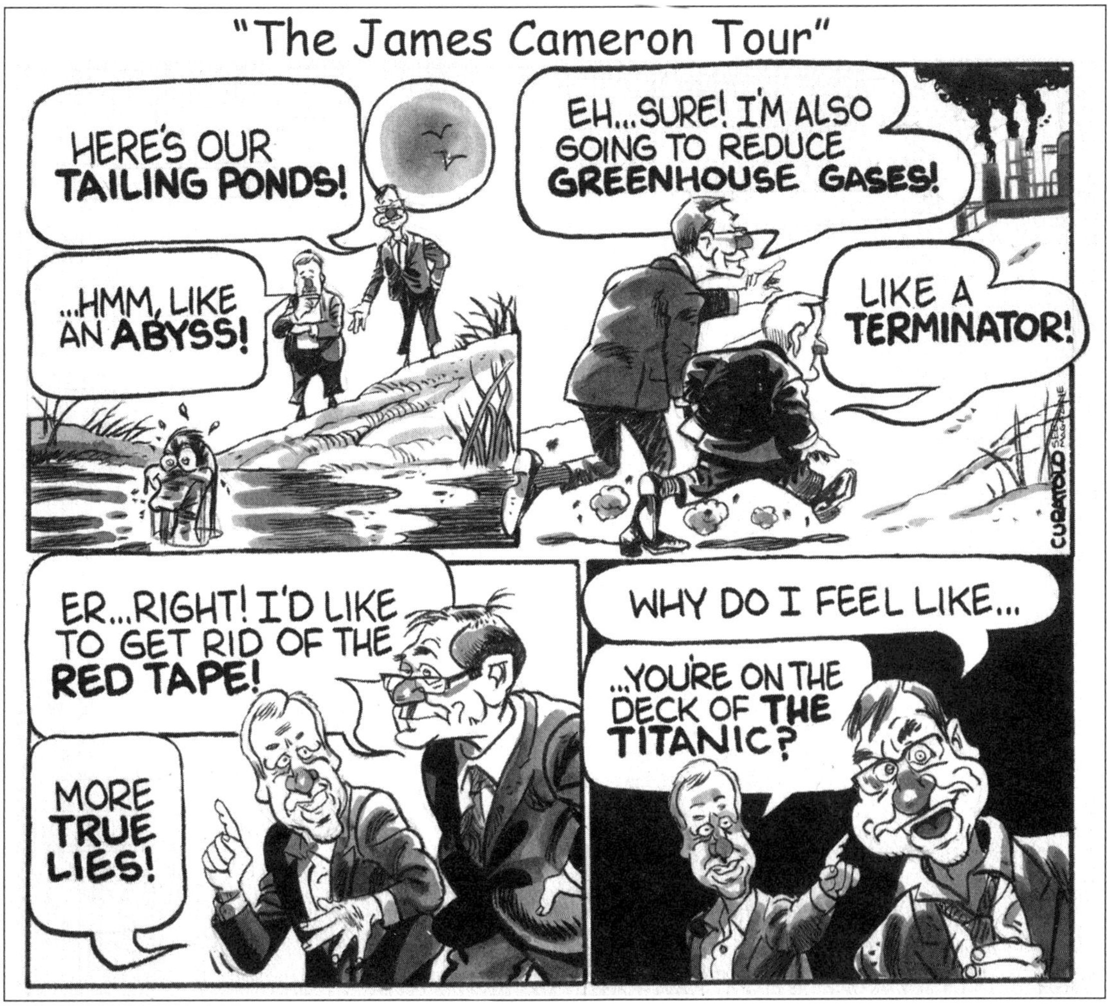
"The James Cameron Tour"
HERE'S OUR TAILING PONDS!
...HMM, LIKE AN ABYSS!
EH...SURE! I'M ALSO GOING TO REDUCE GREENHOUSE GASES!
LIKE A TERMINATOR!
CURATOLO
ER...RIGHT! I'D LIKE TO GET RID OF THE RED TAPE!
MORE TRUE LIES!
WHY DO I FEEL LIKE...
...YOU'RE ON THE DECK OF THE TITANIC?

MARK STREETER
Courtesy Savannah Morning News

NATE BEELER
Courtesy Washington Examiner

Crime

Nineteen people were shot, six fatally, during an open meeting hosted by U.S. Rep. Gabrielle Giffords in Tucson, Arizona. A 22-year-old Tucson man, Jared Lee Loughner, was arrested at the scene and charged with the attempted assassination of a member of Congress and the assassination of a federal judge. Some blamed extreme political speech for the attack, and President Obama called on both sides to tone down the rhetoric.

Florida mother Casey Anthony was arrested and charged with giving false statements to police, child neglect, and obstructing justice after the disappearance of her daughter, Caylee. Caylee's body was later found in a wooded area near the family's home. Casey was charged with first-degree murder, aggravated child abuse, aggravated manslaughter of a child, and four counts of providing false information to police. The prosecution presented 400 pieces of evidence, but after months of arguments and conflicting testimony, the jury found Casey not guilty of all charges except providing false information.

The managing director of the International Monetary Fund, Dominique Gaston André Strauss-Kahn, was accused of sexual assault by a maid. Strauss-Kahn, a French economist, lawyer, and politician, admitted the incident was "inappropriate" and a "moral fault," but denied that the case involved violence or constraint. Officials dropped all charges after the maid's credibility came into question.

BRUCE PLANTE
Courtesy Tulsa World

CHRIS BRITT
Courtesy State Journal-Register (Ill.)

FRED MULHEARN
Courtesy The Advocate (La.)

TOM STIGLICH
Courtesy Northeast Times (Pa.)

DAN CARINO
Courtesy THECARTOONMOVEMENT.COM

DAN CARINO
Courtesy THECARTOONMOVEMENT.COM

BOB UNELL
Courtesy Kansas City Star

TIMOTHY JACKSON
Courtesy Chicago Defender

DAVID HITCH
Courtesy Telegram & Gazette (Mass.)

KEVIN SIERS
Courtesy Charlotte Observer

CHAN LOWE
Courtesy Tribune Media

ANNETTE BALESTERI
Courtesy The News (Calif.)

Space/Air Travel

Several times during the year air traffic controllers were found asleep on the job. Transportation Secretary Ray LaHood declared, "I am totally outraged by these incidents." The sleepers were suspended pending an investigation by the Federal Aviation Administration. The FAA and the Department of Transportation announced that additional air traffic controllers would be added to the night shift at airports where only one person was working.

A small crew of just four astronauts—Christopher Ferguson, Douglas Hurley, Sandra Magnus, and Rex Walheim—flew the 135th and last space shuttle mission aboard *Atlantis*. The shuttle was launched on July 8 and landed safely at Kennedy Space Center on July 21. *Discovery* was the first of NASA's space shuttles to be retired.

The end of the shuttle program, however, does not necessarily mean the end of NASA or sending humans into space. NASA is designing and building capabilities to send humans to explore the solar system, working toward a goal of landing a crew on Mars.

A defunct six-ton satellite passed over the West Coast and near New Zealand before burning up over a remote area of the Pacific Ocean. The 20-year-old satellite dropped about 24 pieces of metal as it entered Earth's atmosphere.

JOSEPH O'MAHONEY
Courtesy The Patriot Ledger

ED STEIN
Courtesy EDSTEININK.COM

TOM STIGLICH
Courtesy Northeast Times (Pa.)

ROSS GOSSE
Courtesy EDITOONS,:NCK

184

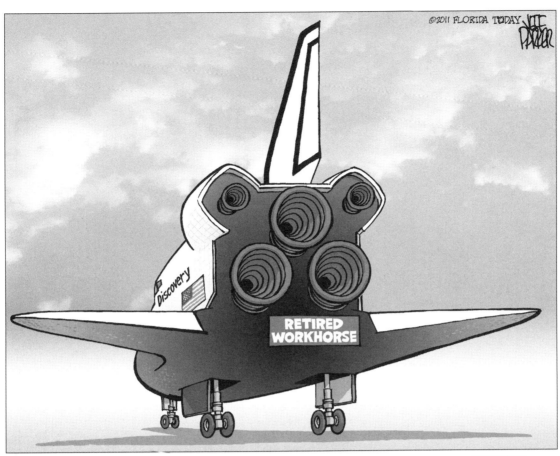

JEFF PARKER
Courtesy Florida Today

NATE BEELER
Courtesy Washington Examiner

CHARLIE DANIEL
Courtesy Knoxville News-Sentinel

BOB UNELL
Courtesy Kansas City Star

DAVID DONAR
Courtesy donarfilms

CHIP BOK
Courtesy Creators Syndicate

RICHARD E. LOCHER
Courtesy Tribune Media Services

CHUCK ASAY
Courtesy Creators.com

LISA BENSON
Courtesy Washington Post Writers Group

...and Other Issues

Wisconsin Gov. Scott Walker touched off a national debate over public employee unions when he tried to solve the state's budget crisis by having workers contribute more to their pension funds and health care. At the heart of the controversy is the right of public employees to engage in collective bargaining. Democrats from the state legislature left the state to avoid voting on the bill.

Scandal rocked the Bureau of Alcohol, Tobacco, Firearms, and Explosives when details of the controversial program dubbed "Fast and Furious" became known. Under the program, thousands of guns ended up in the hands of Mexican cartel members.

The National Labor Relations Board sued Boeing for opening a plant in South Carolina. The suit claimed Boeing was punishing union workers by building in a right-to-work state. House Republicans launched a probe of the bankruptcy of Solyndra, a solar energy company that received more than $500 million in federal loan guarantees as part of President Obama's green jobs initiative. Obama had earlier touted Solyndra as a success story for a green economy.

The cash-strapped U.S. Postal Service announced it was considering canceling Saturday delivery, and the nation marked the 10th anniversary of the 9/11 terrorist attacks. Among notables who died during the year were suicide advocate Dr. Jack Kevorkian, actor James Arness of TV's "Gunsmoke," and saxophonist Clarence Clemons.

PHIL HANDS
Courtesy Wisconsin State Journal

189

SCOTT STANTIS
Courtesy Chicago Tribune

BRUCE QUAST
Courtesy Rockford Register-Star

ED GAMBLE
Courtesy King Features Syndicate

JIM BUSH
Courtesy Providence Journal

JOE RANK
Courtesy Times-Press-Recorder (Calif.)

DAVE COVERLY
Courtesy Creators Syndicate

ED STEIN
Courtesy EDSTEININK.COM

WILLIAM WARREN
Courtesy Liberty Features Syndicate

PAUL FELL
Courtesy Artizans Syndicate

STEVEN PARRA
Courtesy Fresno Bee

MIKE KEEFE
Courtesy Denver Post

CHUCK ASAY
Courtesy Creators.com

JEFF DANZIGER
Courtesy NYTS/CWS

IRENE OLDS
Courtesy The Democrat (Ind.)

JEFF STAHLER
Courtesy Columbus Dispatch

MIKE BECKOM
Courtesy beckomtoonz@aol.com

LYNN CARLSON and BILL SMITH
Courtesy Lompoc Record

JOE HELLER
Courtesy Green Bay Press-Gazette

JEFF DARCY
Courtesy The Plain Dealer (Oh.)

JIM MCCLOSKEY
Courtesy The News-Leader (Va.)

DOUG MACGREGOR
Courtesy The News-Press (Fla.)

JEFF STAHLER
Courtesy Columbus Dispatch

MICHAEL RAMIREZ
Courtesy Investors Business Daily

DANIEL FENECH
Courtesy Heritage Newspapers

MIKE KEEFE
Courtesy Denver Post

GEORGE DANBY
Courtesy Bangor Daily News

JOHN ROSE
Courtesy Byrd Newspapers of Virginia

TOM STIGLICH
Courtesy Northeast Times (Pa.)

BRUCE QUAST
Courtesy Rockford Register-Star

Past Award Winners

PULITZER PRIZE

1922—Rollin Kirby, New York World
1923—No award given
1924—J.N. Darling, New York Herald-Tribune
1925—Rollin Kirby, New York World
1926—D.R. Fitzpatrick, St. Louis Post-Dispatch
1927—Nelson Harding, Brooklyn Eagle
1928—Nelson Harding, Brooklyn Eagle
1929—Rollin Kirby, New York World
1930—Charles Macauley, Brooklyn Eagle
1931—Edmund Duffy, Baltimore Sun
1932—John T. McCutcheon, Chicago Tribune
1933—H.M. Talburt, Washington Daily News
1934—Edmund Duffy, Baltimore Sun
1935—Ross A. Lewis, Milwaukee Journal
1936—No award given
1937—C.D. Batchelor, New York Daily News
1938—Vaughn Shoemaker, Chicago Daily News
1939—Charles G. Werner, Daily Oklahoman
1940—Edmund Duffy, Baltimore Sun
1941—Jacob Burck, Chicago Times
1942—Herbert L. Block, NEA
1943—Jay N. Darling, New York Herald-Tribune
1944—Clifford K. Berryman, Washington Star
1945—Bill Mauldin, United Features Syndicate
1946—Bruce Russell, Los Angeles Times
1947—Vaughn Shoemaker, Chicago Daily News
1948—Reuben L. ("Rube") Goldberg, New York Sun
1949—Lute Pease, Newark Evening News
1950—James T. Berryman, Washington Star
1951—Reginald W. Manning, Arizona Republic
1952—Fred L. Packer, New York Mirror
1953—Edward D. Kuekes, Cleveland Plain Dealer
1954—Herbert L. Block, Washington Post
1955—Daniel R. Fitzpatrick, St. Louis Post-Dispatch
1956—Robert York, Louisville Times
1957—Tom Little, Nashville Tennessean
1958—Bruce M. Shanks, Buffalo Evening News
1959—Bill Mauldin, St. Louis Post-Dispatch
1960—No award given
1961—Carey Orr, Chicago Tribune
1962—Edmund S. Valtman, Hartford Times
1963—Frank Miller, Des Moines Register
1964—Paul Conrad, Denver Post
1965—No award given
1966—Don Wright, Miami News
1967—Patrick B. Oliphant, Denver Post

1968—Eugene Gray Payne, Charlotte Observer
1969—John Fischetti, Chicago Daily News
1970—Thomas F. Darcy, Newsday
1971—Paul Conrad, Los Angeles Times
1972—Jeffrey K. MacNelly, Richmond News Leader
1973—No award given
1974—Paul Szep, Boston Globe
1975—Garry Trudeau, Universal Press Syndicate
1976—Tony Auth, Philadelphia Enquirer
1977—Paul Szep, Boston Globe
1978—Jeff MacNelly, Richmond News Leader
1979—Herbert Block, Washington Post
1980—Don Wright, Miami News
1981—Mike Peters, Dayton Daily News
1982—Ben Sargent, Austin American-Statesman
1983—Dick Locher, Chicago Tribune
1984—Paul Conrad, Los Angeles Times
1985—Jeff MacNelly, Chicago Tribune
1986—Jules Feiffer, Universal Press Syndicate
1987—Berke Breathed, Washington Post Writers Group
1988—Doug Marlette, Atlanta Constitution
1989—Jack Higgins, Chicago Sun-Times
1990—Tom Toles, Buffalo News
1991—Jim Borgman, Cincinnati Enquirer
1992—Signe Wilkinson, Philadelphia Daily News
1993—Steve Benson, Arizona Republic
1994—Michael Ramirez, Memphis Commercial Appeal
1995—Mike Luckovich, Atlanta Constitution
1996—Jim Morin, Miami Herald
1997—Walt Handelsman, New Orleans Times-Picayune
1998—Steve Breen, Asbury Park Press
1999—David Horsey, Seattle Post-Intelligencer
2000—Joel Pett, Lexington Herald-Leader
2001—Ann Telnaes, Tribune Media Services
2002—Clay Bennett, Christian Science Monitor
2003—David Horsey, Seattle Post-Intelligencer
2004—Matt Davies, The Journal News
2005—Nick Anderson, Louisville Courier-Journal
2006—Mike Luckovich, Atlanta Journal-Constitution
2007—Walt Handelsman, Newsday
2008—Michael Ramirez, Investors Business Daily
2009—Steve Breen, San Diego Tribune
2010- Mark Fiore, SFGate.com
2011—Mike Keefe, Denver Post

SIGMA DELTA CHI AWARD

1942—Jacob Burck, Chicago Times
1943—Charles Werner, Chicago Sun
1944—Henry Barrow, Associated Press
1945—Reuben L. Goldberg, New York Sun
1946—Dorman H. Smith, NEA
1947—Bruce Russell, Los Angeles Times
1948—Herbert Block, Washington Post
1949—Herbert Block, Washington Post
1950—Bruce Russell, Los Angeles Times
1951—Herbert Block, Washington Post and
      Bruce Russell, Los Angeles Times
1952—Cecil Jensen, Chicago Daily News
1953—John Fischetti, NEA
1954—Calvin Alley, Memphis Commercial Appeal
1955—John Fischetti, NEA
1956—Herbert Block, Washington Post
1957—Scott Long, Minneapolis Tribune
1958—Clifford H. Baldowski, Atlanta Constitution
1959—Charles G. Brooks, Birmingham News
1960—Dan Dowling, New York Herald-Tribune
1961—Frank Interlandi, Des Moines Register
1962—Paul Conrad, Denver Post
1963—William Mauldin, Chicago Sun-Times
1964—Charles Bissell, Nashville Tennessean
1965—Roy Justus, Minneapolis Star
1966—Patrick Oliphant, Denver Post
1967—Eugene Payne, Charlotte Observer
1968—Paul Conrad, Los Angeles Times
1969—William Mauldin, Chicago Sun-Times
1970—Paul Conrad, Los Angeles Times
1971—Hugh Haynie, Louisville Courier-Journal
1972—William Mauldin, Chicago Sun-Times
1973—Paul Szep, Boston Globe
1974—Mike Peters, Dayton Daily News
1975—Tony Auth, Philadelphia Enquirer

1976—Paul Szep, Boston Globe
1977—Don Wright, Miami News
1978—Jim Borgman, Cincinnati Enquirer
1979—John P. Trever, Albuquerque Journal
1980—Paul Conrad, Los Angeles Times
1981—Paul Conrad, Los Angeles Times
1982—Dick Locher, Chicago Tribune
1983—Rob Lawlor, Philadelphia Daily News
1984—Mike Lane, Baltimore Evening Sun
1985—Doug Marlette, Charlotte Observer
1986—Mike Keefe, Denver Post
1987—Paul Conrad, Los Angeles Times
1988—Jack Higgins, Chicago Sun-Times
1989—Don Wright, Palm Beach Post
1990—Jeff MacNelly, Chicago Tribune
1991—Walt Handelsman, New Orleans Times-
      Picayune
1992—Robert Ariail, Columbia State
1993—Herbert Block, Washington Post
1994—Jim Borgman, Cincinnati Enquirer
1995—Michael Ramirez, Memphis Commercial
      Appeal
1996—Paul Conrad, Los Angeles Times
1997—Michael Ramirez, Los Angeles Times
1998—Jack Higgins, Chicago Sun-Times
1999—Mike Thompson, Detroit Free Press
2000—Nick Anderson, Louisville Courier-Journal
2001—Clay Bennett, Christian Science Monitor
2002—Mike Thompson, Detroit Free Press
2003—Steve Sack, Minneapolis Star-Tribune
2004—John Sherffius, jsherffius@aol.com
2005—Mike Luckovich, Atlanta Journal-Constitution
2006—Mike Lester, Rome News-Tribune
2007—Michael Ramirez, Investors Business Daily
2008—Chris Britt, State Journal-Register
2009—Jack Ohman, The Oregonian
2010—Stephanie McMillan, Code Green

Index of Cartoonists

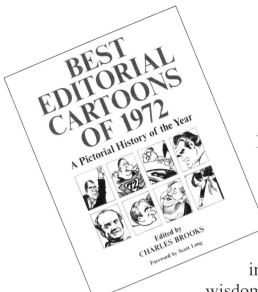

Complete Your CARTOON COLLECTION

Previous editions of this timeless classic are available for those wishing to update their collection of the most provocative moments of the past four decades. Most important, in the end, the wit and wisdom of the editorial cartoonists prevail on the pages of these op-ed editorials, where one can find memories and much, much more in the work of the nation's finest cartoonists.

Select from the following supply of past editions

____1972 Edition	$20.00 pb (F)	____1987 Edition	$20.00 pb	____2001 Edition	$20.00 pb
____1974 Edition	$20.00 pb (F)	____1988 Edition	$20.00 pb	____2002 Edition	$14.95 pb
____1975 Edition	$20.00 pb (F)	____1989 Edition	$20.00 pb (F)	____2003 Edition	$14.95 pb
____1976 Edition	$20.00 pb (F)	____1990 Edition	$20.00 pb	____2004 Edition	$14.95 pb
____1977 Edition	$20.00 pb (F)	____1991 Edition	$20.00 pb	____2005 Edition	$14.95 pb
____1978 Edition	$20.00 pb (F)	____1992 Edition	$20.00 pb	____2006 Edition	$14.95 pb
____1979 Edition	$20.00 pb (F)	____1993 Edition	$20.00 pb	____2007 Edition	$14.95 pb
____1980 Edition	$20.00 pb (F)	____1994 Edition	$20.00 pb	____2008 Edition	$14.95 pb
____1981 Edition	$20.00 pb (F)	____1995 Edition	$20.00 pb	____2009 Edition	$14.95 pb
____1982 Edition	$20.00 pb (F)	____1996 Edition	$20.00 pb	____2010 Edition	$14.95 pb
____1983 Edition	$20.00 pb (F)	____1997 Edition	$20.00 pb	____2011 Edition	$14.95 pb
____1984 Edition	$20.00 pb (F)	____1998 Edition	$20.00 pb		
____1985 Edition	$20.00 pb (F)	____1999 Edition	$20.00 pb	____Add me to the list of standing	
____1986 Edition	$20.00 pb (F)	____2000 Edition	$20.00 pb	orders	

Please include $2.95 for 4th Class Postage and handling or $6.85 for UPS Ground Shipment plus $.75 for each additional copy ordered.

Total enclosed: _____

NAME _____

ADDRESS _____

CITY _____ STATE _____ ZIP _____

Make checks payable to:

PELICAN PUBLISHING COMPANY
1000 Burmaster St, Dept. 6BEC
Gretna, Louisiana 70053-2246

CREDIT CARD ORDERS CALL 1-800-843-1724 or or go to pelicanpub.com
Jefferson Parish residents add 8¾% tax. All other Louisiana residents add 4% tax.
Please visit our Web site at www.pelicanpub.com or e-mail us at sales@pelicanpub.com